Pete Kni
The Cowboy King

by

Darrell Knight

DETSELIG
ENTERPRISES LTD

Pete Knight: The Cowboy King

© 2004 Darrell Knight

Library and Archives Canada Cataloguing in Publication

Knight, Darrell
    Pete Knight : the cowboy king/Darrell Knight.

ISBN 1-55059-274-2 (bound).–ISBN 1-55059-266-1 (pbk.)

    1. Knight, Pete, 1904-1937. 2. Rodeo performers–Alberta–
Biography. 3. Cowboys–Alberta–Biography. I. Title.

GV1833.6.K54K54 2004   791.8'4'092   C2004-902966-5

Detselig Enterprises Ltd.
210, 1220 Kensington Road NW
Calgary, Alberta T2N 3P5

Phone: (403) 283-0900
Fax: (403) 283-6947
Email: temeron@telusplanet.net
www.temerondetselig.com

We acknowledge the support of the Government of Canada through the Book Publishing Industry Development Program (BPIDP) for our publishing program.

We also acknowledge the support of the Alberta Foundation for the Arts for our publishing program.

The Alberta Foundation for the Arts

Alberta COMMUNITY DEVELOPMENT

COMMITTED TO THE DEVELOPMENT OF CULTURE AND THE ARTS

SAN 113-0234
Printed in Canada

Facing photo: Pete and Babe Knight
The Harold Knight Collection
Cover photo: Pete Knight on Counterfit, 1930
The Glenbow Archives

Dedication

To my Parents, Ray and Florence Knight

to Richard and Cindy-Lee

to Sara
so you will also know

to John 'Tuffy' Wurtz and the Deerfield Hutterite Colony
for always remembering

and to Barb

Contents

Acknowledgments

I have many people to thank for assisting in taking this literary work from an idea to a published reality. This book was written as a tribute to a great hero who belonged to and was revered by an entire generation of people in municipalities across western Canada and the United States of America.

My parents, Ray and Florence Knight, offered their encouragement in writing this book; my father provided many hours of reliable, thoughtful recollections of Pete Knight after having had months of close contact long ago with his legendary uncle. My Great-Aunt, Mrs. Ida Lee 'Babe' Knight of Hot Springs, Arkansas, spent many hours relating details of the five years of marriage she cherished with bronc riding legend Pete Knight, during her visits to my parents' home in Calgary. Nellie McClain provided many hours of reminiscences of her famous brother, Pete Knight. Harold and Hilda Knight of Airdrie, Alberta, provided many hours of family reminiscences from early contact with Pete Knight from the 1920's and 30's. Harold also provided never before published photographs of Pete and Babe Knight. Theodore 'Teddy' Togstead, owner of the Deep Dale Ranch at Crossfield, Alberta, provided a summary of Pete Knight's early association with the Deep Dale Ranch.

Journalist Fred Kennedy granted interviews at his Calgary home during the early 1980's, for which I am truly grateful; Fred also provided me with a copy of his book entitled *The Calgary Stampede Story*, for research. The interviews provided by rodeo contestants Frank Sharp and Dick West – both good friends of Pete Knight's – were of invaluable assistance in providing an insight into the colorful early stampede era in Alberta. American ProRodeo Hall of Fame inductee, Harry Vold of Colorado Springs, a close friend of the legendary bronc rider Harry Knight and a spokesman for rodeo contestants from an earlier era, provided interviews by telephone and in person, which could not have taken place without the kind assistance of sons Wayne and Doug Vold, Bucking Horse Stock Contractors of High River, Alberta. They are also members of the Canadian Professional Rodeo Association in Calgary (CPRA). The CPRA Rodeo Administrator Bob Phipps kindly provided the rules of the Bucking Horse event in Canada, as they are adhered to today. Urban Guichon, Owner of Riley & McCormick Saddlery of Calgary, provided interviews and documents pertaining to both the company's involvement with the stampedes in Calgary, and the personalities that stood out from the rest. Mary Guichon provided much information on her father, the former Alderman Eneas

McCormick, who was a founding partner of Riley & McCormick Saddlery in 1901 and a good friend to Pete Knight. Saddle-maker Hank Freisen provided an insight on the personality and reputation of legendary saddle-maker Johnny Foss, who plied his trade at Riley & McCormick for over forty years and created many of the saddles won by Pete Knight. Assistant Curator Doug Cass, Cultural Historian Lorain Lounsberry and reference archivist Harry Sanders, all of Calgary's Glenbow Museum, provided photographic images, encouragement and further examination of Pete Knight effects held in the Glenbow Museum collection; none of which could have been accessed without their expert assistance and guidance.

Calgarian Tom Williams, noted seller of antique books, provided required research material. Cliff Ball, of Olathe (Kansas) Historical Society, provided insight on the C.H. HYER & SONS Boot Company. Gerry Silliker, of the University of Calgary, provided technical assistance and computer expertise in the preparation of the manuscript, and the manuscript itself could not have been prepared without the functional assistance and guidance of Merlin Keillor and Judy Smith, of the Nat Christie Adaptive Technology Centre, University of Calgary.

Special thanks is overdue to Dr. Anne McWhir, Dr. Margaret Hadley, Dr. Stephen Guy-Bray, Dr. Jason Weins, Dr. Jackie Jenkins, all of the Department of English, University of Calgary, for the collective encouragement that brought this project to fruition. Glenda Magallon, of the University of Calgary's Mackimmie Library, arranged for research material to be brought from other Libraries. Dr. Aubrey Levin of the Peter Lougheed Centre, Calgary, provided encouragement and publishing insight. Robert Kroetsch, author of *Seed Catalogue* (Winnipeg: Turnstone Press, 2001), provided a literary medium which prompted me to write about the legend and myth of Pete Knight; for Mr. Kroetsch's personal encouragement, I am humbly grateful. Cliff Faulknor, author of Herman Linder's biography entitled *Turn Him Loose*, provided knowledgeable insight into another Alberta rodeo legend who was a close friend to Pete Knight. Christine Hayes of the Calgary Public Library assisted with access to the Wilf Carter Archive material held therein.

Archivist Mona Reno of the Nevada State Library in Carson City provided material from the Pony Express Days of 1932, and Barbara Bunshah and Loretta Cordrey of the Livermore Heritage Guild provided historical material pertaining to Pete Knight. Alice Hanks Allen of the Montana Western musical group "Saddle-Bags" supplied lyrics from Wilf Carter's repertoire. Mark Simpson provided advice, computer expertise, and downloading of archive material. Marianne, Sonny and C.J. Beauregard – all of the Harry Rowell family of Hayward, California – provided valuable resource material. Nanette Hyer Bohl and Charles Hyer, both of the C.H. HYER family provided valuable insight into their grandfather's famous boot company. Peggy Haskell and Jim Svoboda provided small pieces to a vast puzzle from Burwell, Nebraska. Bruce K. Lee, Chief Executive Officer of the Pete Knight Memorial Foundation in Bluffton Arkansas, scouted for information on Pete Knight's rodeo performances in Australia and the southern United States. From the National Cowboy and Western Heritage Museum, Oklahoma City, where Pete Knight's trophies have been enshrined for half a century, Richard Rattenbury, Curator of History assisted in providing a myriad of information on rodeos where the famous bronc rider competed. The many staff members of the ProRodeo Hall of Fame and Museum of the American Cowboy in Colorado Springs where Pete Knight is a founding honoree, also offered their generous assistance and support. Daughter and son-in-law of Alberta bronc rider Jimmy Moony, Sharon and Herm Theilen, provided invaluable archival material and photographic images pertaining to the Alberta Stampede Company and to Pete Knight. Joe Bruisedhead of Card-ston provided unflagging assistance, in providing a brief historical summary of his father, the legendary Native bronc rider Pete Bruisedhead.

I must also include a special note of thanks to my editor, Kim-Marie Robertson, who spent many hours reading and correcting the first drafts of the Pete Knight manuscript. To those others who helped with details large and small too numerous to mention, thank you all.

Preface

In 1957, twenty years after Pete Knight's sudden death, I was born in Calgary and raised on a mixed cattle-grain farm in southern Alberta in the heart of 'Pete Knight' country. My paternal grandfather, Robert Knight of Irricana, Alberta, was Pete Knight's oldest brother. The Knight family was a very close-knit entity at the height of my great-uncle's fame. The Knights were grain farmers, not ranchers, and certainly not cowboys, as successive legends have often depicted. They were American-born, canny rural businessmen who made their living from the sale of wheat and barley gleaned from their farmland with horse-drawn cultivators, seed-drills and threshing machines; all manned by itinerant gangs of seasonally-hired immigrant laborers. It was a matter of quiet, dignified pride for Robert Knight and his brother Walt that their youngest brother, Pete, became one of the most famous men in the Canadian west, and a bronc riding legend across North America.

Wilf Carter's lyrical ballad entitled, "Pete Knight: The King of the Cowboys" was played every week on southern Alberta's radio stations from the 1930's through the 1960's, and I was often asked by curious rural Albertans if I was related to Pete Knight. My teachers at Viscount Torrington School, where I was a pupil during grade school, all knew I was a relative of Pete Knight's, and this seemed to be a good reason for our educators – all of whom had lived in Alberta at the height of Pete Knight's fame – to encourage the singing of 'cowboy songs' in our music classes.

Old cowboys always welcomed me into their homes and, with their eyes gleaming, would regale me with their personal reminiscences of having seen Pete Knight ride bucking horses. The recollection would take these frail old men back to the robust flair of their youth, while the elderly ladies who remembered Pete Knight always recalled his rugged good looks, charm, and respectful manners. He was, without any doubt, a 'gentleman's gentleman.' At a country wedding near Sundre, Alberta, I was introduced as "Pete Knight's grandnephew," by the bride's paternal grandfather. He was an old cowboy who had worked the Calgary Stampede chutes in the 1920's and knew my family. Elderly, arthritic cowboys stood and grasped my hand with all the strength each could muster and uttered with the greatest sincerity, "I am honored to meet you." In each case, it was clear the speaker meant it.

Pete Knight had been and would always be their greatest hero, and I understood the solemn weight of responsibility that I carried on behalf of the late, great Pete Knight.

From the time I was five years old, while accompanying my Dad to cattle sales and auction barns across southern Alberta, old cowboys who knew my father looked down at me and with a wistful but proud look of recollection, would state, "Yes, I knew your Great-uncle Pete…he sure was a swell guy!" These men insisted on paying for soft drinks and candy bars at the all-male country gatherings, for they "couldn't do enough" for a relative of the legendary bronc rider.

The cattle and bucking horse auctions are held today across southern Alberta as they were in my youth, and as they had been when Pete Knight rode bucking horses. The dusty arenas echo with the hurried staccato of the auctioneer's call, and the odors of beef on the hoof, leather whips, and perspiring ring attendants all mingle beneath the close, studied forum of wary, bidding cattlemen. It still transcends all time, harkening back to the days when cattlemen and farmers first arrived in Alberta. The discussion from these quiet, weathered farmers and ranchers often deals with cattle prices, the government . . . and rodeo legends.

Decades later, when I entered a bucking horse contest at the Drumheller Amateur Rodeo, a dozen competing cowboys in the infield began chanting "Darrell Knight's First Ride," alluding to the song Wilf Carter had written fifty years earlier of my Great-uncle Pete's last ride. From a handful of fellow rodeo contestants, it was a tribute expressed in good taste and received in good humour.

Over the years, I encountered a litany of Pete Knight myths and legends – often humorous, but nearly always erroneous – and have met in passing, many people over the years in the most surprising places who emphatically claimed that they too were related to Pete Knight. I would always ask which relative they were married to, or who their 'relative' had been on the Knight side of the family, and always, the supposed relationship would end in uncertainty, confusion, or outright invention. Each new introduction that I had to yet another 'unrelated relative' claiming Pete Knight as his mother's brother or Aunt Freida's distant cousin, was further affirmation to me that Pete Knight's history must one day be written; by a member of his family who heard the stories firsthand from the people who knew him best.

One myth claimed that Pete Knight died while riding *Midnight* at the Calgary Stampede, a myth undoubtedly generated through the painting of the legendary horse and rider, created by western artist Doug Stephens. Another myth has circulated, alluding to Pete Knight being killed while riding the *Strawberry Roan*, a bucking horse from one of Wilf Carter's songs. Other myths, possibly emanating from disgruntled and disenchanted individuals, claim that the Pete Knight phenomenon hadn't been anything special. The truth may never be fully untangled from these, but a common thread runs through the fabric of the tales often repeated: Pete Knight *is* remembered and was a name to be reckoned with. All that remains of the intangible rumors and stories told of this great western hero are just that . . . myths.

Pete Knight was the most accomplished bronc rider of the twentieth century, and the greatest hero that Alberta ever had or may ever have again. The evidence is unequivocal. Three generations of cowboys, ranchers, farmers and business owners have extended unreserved friendship, hospitality and kindness; all because of how each of these many people felt about their bronc-riding hero, Pete Knight. The goodwill that has been extended to my family in all of the rodeo regions of western Canada and the United States of America during the last eighty years can never be repaid. This work is a tribute to my great-uncle, who was the acclaimed 'King of the Cowboys' of the 1930s, the legendary Pete Knight. The book was written to dispel the myths and rumors surrounding his life and legend, and to thank all of his friends and his many fans – mostly rodeo cowboys – who have never forgotten the name of Pete Knight and the man he became.

Prologue

Heavy rains had fallen for more than a week, blanketing the rolling, grassy hills and fields being prepared for spring seeding across southern Alberta. The weather, in retrospect, was sent to herald the coming of ominous tidings on that May week-end in 1937. As rain poured, thunder rolled and lighting slashed across the expanse of the prairies, the ringing of an oak wall-mounted telephone broke the reverie of the weather-watchers at my grandfather's farm, ten miles east of Crossfield, Alberta. My father, Raymond, was closest to the telephone and took the call. The identity of the caller could not be remembered in the years that followed, but the caller's message was burned into the memory of the thirteen-year-old who answered the telephone that afternoon. Pete Knight, Alberta's premier World Champion Bucking Horse rider had been killed that day at a rodeo in Hayward, California, while riding before a packed stadium of five thousand spectators.

Young Raymond was stunned by the ill-fated news. "The man's calling from California!" he cried out to all in the household. "He said Uncle Pete was killed today!" The teenager held the receiver in a shaking hand, and sent his younger siblings scurrying to bring their father to the telephone.

Robert broke down and immediately began to cry. He could not speak to the caller. Pete's only other brother, Walter Knight, lived three miles away and did not have a telephone. In a flurry of haste driven by the sudden news of the tragedy, Raymond's older brother, Bob, raced in a grain truck to Walt's farm and brought his uncle back to verify the content of the call.

The Knights were not only obligated to attend their brother's funeral, they wanted to be in attendance, but money was scarce. On the weight of a handshake, neighbor Herb Stewart financed the trip to California for Rob and Walt Knight. The money would be repaid, when it became available. Family friend and neighboring farmer, Archie Heines, went with the Knight boys as a third driver. In the days that followed, Robert, Walt and Archie drove nonstop in Walt's aging 1928 Chevrolet Sedan, from Crossfield to California. After making a series of wrong turns and backtrack routings on the primitive highway system that served the American mountain states in the 1930s, and disheveled by three days and nights of bouncing non-stop over rough roads at an average of fifty-five miles per hour, lack of adequate food or sleep, and the changing of several blown tires, the three somber men finally arrived in Hayward – an hour after the solemn ceremony had ended. Prior to the bronc rider's burial, the coffin was reopened and a private service was afforded to the Knight brothers and their travelling companion, along with Pete's wife, Babe, and their only daughter also in attendance. Pete Knight was laid to rest in the Lone Tree cemetery on the outskirts of grief-stricken Hayward.

The owner of Hayward's renowned rodeo, Harry Rowell, paid for Pete's funeral and for his cemetery plot at Lone Tree: the expense and logistical difficulty of hauling a lead-lined coffin and body across four states and an international border was an impracticality reserved only for the very rich. With reverence to the legendary symbol of horsemanship, athletic competition, and goodwill that Pete Knight had become, the businesses in that no-nonsense California ranching centre closed for an entire week. Other firms across the length and breadth of North America followed suit, all paying tribute to the man who had truly become the King of the Cowboys– in legend, in song and indelibly, in their hearts.

Tragedy had not just struck the Knight family or the Rodeo world – a sense of throat-gripping shock and sadness was felt from Australia to England, from Alberta to Texas, and especially for every competitor in a rodeo arena, anywhere in North America. Pete Knight, like many noble kings, died a hero's death beneath the hooves of a rank, wild bucking horse, at the centre stage of the sport the great Alberta rodeo rider had devoted his life to for more than two decades. The King would die a mortal death, but his legend would be elevated to one of near deity. His feats of prowess while riding *Midnight* and other renowned bucking horses would be told and retold in the decades to follow. Around campfires and in city saloons, on cattle drives and played on country radio stations across North America, the legend of Pete Knight was destined to live forever.

1

Beginnings

It may be accurately stated that the far-reaching reputation of Pete Knight began on the afternoon of Friday, July 11, 1924, at the world-famous Calgary Stampede. More than a dozen semi-finalists had drawn the names of their bucking horses, and each spurred his assigned bronc out past the plane of the infield chutes, one after the other. At the end of the day, five riders remained in competition against one another, in a contest where all others had been bucked off or otherwise disqualified. The mounted finalists stood in a serried rank, cheered on by the grandstand crowd as the Stampede's official photographer, William J. Oliver, captured their photographic images. With Stetsons in hand, and their rough, wooly angora chaps contrasting with stiff-boiled dress shirts, the five young men: Pete Seeley, Cecil Henley, Pete La Grandeur, Bayse Collins and a recent up-and-coming arrival to professional bucking horse competition, Pete Knight – smiled and waved back to the crowd. The following afternoon would see those five riders compete in the Calgary Stampede's premier contest, the bucking horse event with saddle. At stake was the most prestigious sporting award in Canada, known to every rider across the west simply as the Prince's Cup.

When the horses were bucked out and the points tallied up, Seeley, Henley and Collins were disqualified. Pete La Grandeur won the event, the trophy, and the prize money that went with it, but Pete Knight finished in second place behind La Grandeur by less than a fraction of a point. It was the first professional recognition that Pete Knight would receive – and he would be showered with still more – in a career that would bring him fame, honor, wealth and legendary status over the next thirteen years of his life. He would be long remembered in the decades following his death, but even great men have humble beginnings.

Pete's father and my paternal great-grandfather, William Knight, was raised in Kingman County, Kansas, United States of America, in the 1870's. In an era of horse-drawn power, William had been trained as a horseman and lay-veterinarian of indisputable ability and reputation. On a continent where most goods were pulled or carried by horses, an enterprising young man with the ability to handle horses responsibly could go far.

Although raised in the United States, William was born in Stockport, England, to a family of Knights who held military service and biblical studies in high regard. At an early age, he and his two brothers were brought to America by their father, Peter Knight. Few records exist today to tell of Peter senior's life in England or of his decision to move his family to the United States; however, it is known that he could neither read nor write. When Peter received a letter from family members in England, young William would read the letter to his father, and Peter would commit the letter to memory. Years afterward, he was able to recite the content of these numerous letters, verbatim.

Kansas was a state bordering the frontier, serviced by a new railroad from the east and was the interim destination in 1885 for tens of thousands of range cattle being trail-driven to market. Destination centres such as Dodge City had been raised on the rolling grasslands of this new state, and immigrant settlement was gradually driving the cowboys, gunfighters and whisky towns to new frontiers. It was against the backdrop of this setting that William met and married Irish-born Katherine Carson, in 1884, at Kingman. Their first-born was Robert Knight, who arrived in 1885 and whose birth was registered at the local county courthouse. In 1887, William moved his new family to the bustling city of Philadelphia, to enter into the weaving trade in that booming American centre. William's father and two unmarried brothers left Kansas at the same time, striking out for the new state of Oklahoma and the free land being offered there for homesteaders, in what would become known as 'the Oklahoma Land Runs.'

For more than fifteen years, William operated a loom in a Philadelphia textiles factory, as his sons and daughters arrived and the family increased in size. Walt was the next born, followed by Maggie, Anna, and Nellie. On May 5, 1903, the Knight family welcomed into the world their newest member and the sixth born to William and Katherine . On the day of his birth at the family's home on Willow Street, he was named Peter Charles Knight, in honor of his paternal grandfather.

William Knight was not an easy parent to get along with. Although of sober habit, he had a short fuse and a fierce temper when provoked, and was not afraid to vent his anger on sons, daughters or bystanders. When the family was feeling the wrath of his foul mood, the Knight brothers and sisters were able to gauge the depth of William's ire by how far his shaggy eye-brows were drooping over his eyes. On one occasion, Walt was hidden in a closet and fed by his younger siblings for two days, after one of Walt's many indiscretions caused William to go on the warpath. After yet another incident, William locked Walt out of the family home, forcing the boy to live rough for two days with a neighborhood urchin. In the course of time, Walt outgrew his scrappy nature and matured to become a shrewd and responsible businessman. Little Pete remained the darling of the family, and was doted on by his brothers and sisters, a determinant that contributed greatly to the mild nature that Pete would carry through adolescence into manhood. While Katherine was busy preparing supper for the family, Anna, Maggie, and Nellie would all take turns rocking little Pete in his crib, as well as feeding and dressing him. It was at that time that William bought Pete his first horse – a sturdy, hardwood rocking horse with a mane and tail of real horsehair, with a brightly painted saddle and a genuine cowhide bridle to match. While the sounds of the city echoed beyond the Knight family's front door, Pete could be found at any given hour of the day, quietly studying the intricacies of balance and the use of the horse's mane, while practicing on his rocking horse in the parlor of his parents's Philadelphia home.

William, beset with a constant, troubling restlessness again experienced a bout of 'itchy feet' and before long the family was relocated to Peter's home-stead in Oklahoma. More than any other occupation of his desire, William wanted to be a farmer, and the 'Cherokee State' was a good place to raise crops and families. Although the Knight children were at first regarded as city-slickers, they caught on quickly as they became familiar with their new surroundings and the farm's livestock. Robert, by that time in his late teens, bought an expensive Surrey to go courting with, much to the objection of his Father, who saw the expenditure as a waste of hard-earned money. The Surrey was a single-horse rig with a convertible top that could be raised or lowered as weather permitted. By any standard of the day this was as fine a vehicle to own as could be found anywhere across the western United States; especially for a young man whose intentions were serious toward his future bride. Robert taught young Pete to harness the horse to his new rig, and to drive the Surrey with adult expertise.

The family farm was of common prosperity in that region of Oklahoma, and the raising of crops – primarily corn, cotton, and garden vegetables – became a family effort, while William bought and sold livestock as his primary occupation. The growing season in Oklahoma for tomatoes was long enough to allow for vine ripening, and the vegetable was fully mature before picking; a fact that Robert would nostalgically refer to many years after while harvesting crops in Alberta's vastly different climate.

Horses were the mainstay of the farm's dray and planting capability, and when Pete was old enough to lift a bucket of corn or reach high enough to curry a horse while standing on a manger beside the haltered animal, he began training himself to ride – first with the assistance of his older siblings and then on his own. It took a minimum of guile to tease a horse into following the boy with the enticement of a bucket of grain. Scarcely more effort was required to slip a rope around the animal's neck and then a halter on his head, as the horse quietly fed on the corn. Without assistance, the young rider was able to clamber aboard the horse's back while the animal was occupied with licking the last kernel from the grain bucket. With a pair of modified reins leading to the rider's hands from the halter-ring, the boy then had control of his mount. After overcoming any initial unsteadiness as the horse plodded around the corral at a slow walk, Pete quickly gained the confidence he needed to urge his horse into a trot, a canter, and eventually a full gallop. Much of what he learned of horsemanship was passed on by his father and older brothers.

Pete was taught never to strike a horse around its head, and to care for the horses and mules on the family farm in a responsible manner. Young Pete loved the horses he rode and cared for, no matter whose horses they were or what their chore might be. The boy took his lessons seriously, and practiced them on a daily basis. The Knight family depended entirely on the well-being of the farm's horses and mules, as all of the vehicles and implements on the farm were horse-drawn. Nothing else mattered as much as the welfare of the farm's livestock, which became as much a primary concern to Pete as it was to his father.

The Knights were doing well in Oklahoma in the first and second decade of the twentieth century and there was no reason for the family to pick up and leave again. Robert had a good job running dray-wagons, and young Pete was learning to drive teams of horses while engaged in the labor of planting and harvesting. Market prices for grain and beef, although not outstanding, were adequate to make a decent living. The family patriarch, however, was again becoming restless, and had already begun looking for another change of scenery.

During a visit to the Oklahoma State Fair, William's attention was drawn to a promotion booth sponsored by the Alberta Government; inexpensive farmland was being advertised by the Albertans, and Oklahomans were being asked to consider immigration to the western Canadian prairie province. Samples of grain, quotations of the generous yield per acre, live exhibits of Alberta's beef and other livestock, photographs of the picturesque Alberta scenery, and proof of a climate that was manageable all served to entice the elderly man. Convincing the rest of the Knight family to leave Oklahoma for a distant, unfamiliar country was going to be a difficult matter. Robert had recently married Anna Wooliver of Stroud, so picking up stakes and leaving for Alberta was not even a remote consideration for the newly-wedded couple. Walt and his other unmarried siblings were skeptical, as they knew nothing of the Canadian west; sister Anna had been proposed to by a young man in Stroud, and she was considering the proposal.

William continued to badger each member of his family into considering a move to western Canada. He had often complained that the climate and conditions of Oklahoma's summers were malarial, and medically debilitating when he suffered from his frequent bouts of ague. His sons and daughters considered this, and the discussion continued. The southern-central United States also suffered from the devastation of annual tornados, a phenomenon that seldom extended north to Alberta's plains. As no one in the family was fully prepared to listen to his entreaties, William – then in his sixties – packed a gunnysack of provisions, said goodbye to his family and clambered aboard the first northbound freight train that would carry him to southern Alberta. Although aging, William often travelled as the railroad brakemen allowed, passing through the itinerant track-side hobo camps and offering some small morsel for the mulligan stew-pot always to be found there.

Within a few months, after making the round-trip, living rough and riding for many hundreds of miles in open boxcars, the Knight patriarch arrived back in Oklahoma at the end of the summer. What he had seen of the opportunity in Alberta shone brightly in his eyes. "Rich, black farmland, with more than a foot of top-soil!" was the picture that William painted of southern Alberta. Fields of chest-high grain rippled in a wavy sea of green and gold, as far as the distant horizon in every direction, and beyond. There were no poisonous snakes to contend with, and the climate was mild yet warm, by any standard. The people were friendly, nearly all of European extraction and few, if any aside from the police, carried a pistol.

Americans, he related, were arriving in Alberta by the tens of thousands, and had been trekking to the territory for more than two decades. The cattle, grain, and conditions of land purchase were all that had been advertised, and more. Furthermore, no immigration application was necessary for any member of the family, as William was British by birth. Canada was a British dominion, and King George V reigned over the dominions; William had long been an ardent fan of this King. Positively gushing with excitement, the tale he related of Alberta's strengths was enough to convince the Knights that William was dead serious about leaving Oklahoma.

In the spring of 1914, William's family began packing up and moving to western Canada. It would be almost three years, however, before the family completed the move to Alberta, as family ties with their Oklahoman relatives remained strong and the harsh Canadian winters initially came as a shock to family members who continued to seasonally travel back and forth to the southern states. Although the Oklahoma farm remained a family possession, livestock was sold at auction in Stroud, and personal effects and heirlooms were crated and shipped by rail to Alberta. William's daughter Anna – the eldest of the three girls – soon married a young man from Stroud by the name of Beeman, and would remain in Oklahoma for the rest of her life.

When the Knight family arrived in Calgary, William, with Robert and Walt assisting, immediately set out to rent farmland for the family, with intent to purchase at a later date. The Knights were advised by land agents from a Calgary real estate firm that If they were considering the purchase of farmland anywhere in Alberta they would do well to buy within a twenty-mile corridor on either side of the north-to-south CPR main rail line, in any community between Calgary and Edmonton.

The first Knight family home north of Calgary was rented from the 'Cap' Wigle family, a dozen miles east of Crossfield near the Rosebud River. It was certainly nothing elaborate, but the 'Wigle place' was a roof overhead and provided an excellent foot-hold to begin putting down permanent roots. Pete, who had not yet finished his grade school studies, attended the Davis School, which bordered on the Rodney School district. The boy from Oklahoma and his classmates at the tiny, one-room schoolhouse would eagerly await the teacher's dismissal of the class each day, anxious for the lessons to end. They would race their saddle ponies to home pastures, with young Pete often winning the contest and the few meager pennies the boys had all wagered.

After initially living under one roof with William, Katherine and their younger siblings, Robert and Walt each took the advice of the real estate agents they had met, and purchased sections of land adjacent the Kersey rural post office, twelve miles southeast of Crossfield. The farms were desirable, and well-situated on gentle, sloping ground, with clean, fast flowing creeks running through the heart of the properties.

The William Knight Family; circa 1914
Photo taken shortly after their arrival in the Crossfield, Alberta district.
From left to right: Robert Knight, Walt Knight, Nellie (Knight) McClain, Pete Knight *(wearing a Stetson)*, Maggie (Knight) Thatcher, William Knight, Anna (Knight) Beeman, Anna (Wooliver) Knight, and Katherine (Carson) Knight.
Photo source: Author

By the summer of 1914, Pete had become an exceptionally good rider despite being only eleven-years-old. To his daily chores, Pete added 'riding the rough' off of the family's several dozen saddle horses. This entailed roping a pony – often one that had been saddled only a few times before – applying a sack over the horse's eyes to calm him, then saddling and bridling the shaking animal in a small corral. Pete would then mount the horse, remove the sack, and turn him out into an open field, allowing the horse to buck or run as he pleased. Eleven years of age was young for a boy to be breaking horses, but Pete was fearless when it came to breaking stray horses found loose on the open range, and a few dollars could be made when he wasn't plowing fields with a team of harness-broken horses.

With the outbreak of the war in Europe during the summer of 1914, Canada's rapidly growing army increased demands for beef, grain, horses – especially mules and hundreds of miles of harness. This demand brought a rapid halt to the recession that western Canada had experienced through the spring and summer of that year. Within ninety days of the army's initial mobilization, the first full division of Canadian army troops sailed for England, accompanied by thousands of horses and mules. As they sailed, a second division of twenty thousand men was already being contemplated.

The Knight family, as most other farming families in the district, began to prosper from the war demand. Farming was essential service in support of the war effort, and the Knight family realized their good fortune that duty at home took precedence over fighting in an overseas war. The Knights counted their blessings, worked their newly-acquired farmland as patriots, and did what they could to support the national effort. While Pete did his part to farm the Wigle quarter, Walt took a job in Calgary driving a horse-drawn hearse for a local funeral parlor.

"The war will be over by Christmas" was the often-expressed sentiment in the autumn of 1914, and it would be much later that the war would be referred to as 'The Great War.' Young men from southern Alberta were enlisting for the army in droves; one of the notable ranchers from Crossfield who had befriended the Knights was Russ Boyle, a former army officer and Boer War veteran. Boyle was promoted to Colonel and given the command of Calgary's overseas-bound 'Tenth Battalion.' In April of 1915, Colonel Boyle, along with more than half of his 'Fighting Tenth' from southern Alberta, lost their lives at Saint Julien's Wood, Belgium, while facing an onslaught of German gas attacks that badly bent but could not break the Canadian line. The loss of Colonel Boyle was acknowledged with pride and sadness by Crossfield district citizens, and was a prompting factor for William Knight to join the army. With patriotic fervor, William offered his services and initially carried a sandwich-board recruiting poster through the streets of Calgary for the army recruiting office. Despite being in his late sixties, William proved his physical ability to man a home-guard position in Alberta's thirteenth military district. He was sworn in and assigned to the horse barns at Sarcee Camp, to be employed as an assistant hostler. At the time, Sarcee was a sprawling complex housing thousands of recruits for the military district on Indian land leased by the army, and many hundreds of horses and mules were being funneled through the camp for overseas duty in Europe.

William was assigned to a barracks and issued a uniform, at which time he assumed his paid duties in the care and feeding of the livestock, harnessing the army's teams and driving the army's wagons. Most hostlers assigned to home-front livestock duty were older men with a sure knowledge of horses and horse ailments; men who assumed a quiet pride in this unsung duty became the backbone of the support for the men fighting overseas. It is not known if William had lied about his age to gain entrance to the army, but what is remembered is that he took service to his king seriously and remained at Sarcee Camp for many months. In addition to his duties at Sarcee, William was also assigned to guard the German Prisoner-of-War Camp located at Seebe, Alberta. On weekends, Katherine Knight, with Pete, Maggie and Nellie, often drove to the distant Prisoner-of-War camp to visit William during his brief Sunday rest.

While his father was serving the colors, Pete, now fourteen years of age, assumed greater responsibility in assisting his brothers with the business of farming. He was rapidly growing into a muscular young man. When Pete wasn't running a horse-drawn one-way plow or seed drill while standing or sitting on the back of the implement and hollering "gee" and "haw" to the harnessed teams pulling him across the black, fertile land, he could be found scooping harvested grain into wagons destined for the Acme elevators. Pete gave his all, with perspiration rolling off his back, and an enduring smile on his face. No matter how hard Pete had to work, he maintained his quiet, pleasant manner in the course of his toil, and was always friendly and polite to everyone he encountered. People tended to like Pete at first meeting.

It was in the brief periods of rest taken after long hours of labor, when Pete would saddle one of his ponies, mount up and take him for a long ride along the Rosebud River. In the first few moments, the horse would set out to dump his rider into the stubble, engaging in a twisting flurry of bone-jarring leaps across the farm field, before Pete could make the animal obey to bridle and spurs. His riding skill had increased to a point where he was seriously training for a formal bucking horse competition, advertised in Crossfield's newspaper, *The Chronicle*, and discussed at length by his neighbors and close friends, that fifth summer of the war. Pete would soon find his opportunity to ride against older, far more experienced bronc riders.

2
The Tools of His Trade

By the summer of 1918, Pete, having turned fifteen that spring, had filled out to a muscular one hundred-sixty pounds. Although standing only five and a half feet tall, he was often mistaken as being older, especially when observed handling horses or pitching barley-stooks on a threshing gang. His youthful but weathered cheeks, tanned dark from daily toil on Alberta's open prairie, had begun to sprout whiskers. With so many men having left the district for overseas duty, there was an unwritten expectation that younger men would fill their places in the labor force, at a younger age. At the end of each work week, the boys in the Davis district sought the camaraderie, challenge, and pure, clean excitement of horse-mounted sporting competition, and for them, that meant riding bucking horses in local competition, usually for quarter-dollar bets.

Pete's formal training as a bronc rider began at the Deep Dale Ranch, just twelve miles east of Crossfield at the confluence of the Rosebud River and the Carstairs Creek. The Ranch was founded in 1910 by Frank Lount, a local Justice of the Peace and business promoter, and was the closest residence to the rented Knight property, being just one mile distant. Lount's foreman was Dave Togstead, a highly-revered gentleman-cowboy, whose reputation for generosity and honesty preceded him across southern Alberta. Togstead could be counted on to assist his neighbors in any way he could, and for his trustworthiness, he was made manager of the area's domestic animal pound. Stray horses and beef cattle were often found wandering the open range, and were delivered on the hoof to the Deep Dale Ranch's impound corral. There, they were fed and watered until the animal's owner could be located or the stray sold at auction. The regional cattle dip – where the area's cattle received treatment for mange – was also located on Lount property, making the ranch a rural meeting point for farmers and ranchers alike.

The cattle dip consisted of a long, descending trench, roughly five feet in the ground at its deepest point. Water was heated in a nearby boiler, and a hot solution of sulphur and lime were mixed into the half-filled defile, which the cattle were then driven through. Great herds of Hereford and Short-horn and Texas Long-horn cattle were driven on the hoof to Lount's cattle dip from many miles away.

Cowboys bringing the herds shared news, provisions, and often entertained themselves with impromptu bucking contests.

On most Sundays during the spring and summer, Pete and a dozen other teenage boys from the area rode their ponies to the Deep Dale Ranch where these informal rodeos were held. Being an expert horseman, Dave Togstead rode in the 'pick-up man' position during the contest, on a big, blue roan he called *Jim*.

Riding pick-up demanded exceptional skill, and the quick response of an obedient, well-trained saddle horse. The pick-up man galloped his horse to a position beside the bucking bronc as the ride ended. After the ten-second gun was fired by a designated judge, who observed the ride from behind the safety of a corral railing, the bronc rider would then scramble onto the back of the pick-up horse, behind the rider's saddle-cantle, and was carried to safety – away from the bucking horse's flying hooves. Pete, Andy Schwartzenberger and many other local boys competed on Togstead's bucking horses or led a horse of their own to the gathering. Togstead offered everyone encouragement and constructive criticism after their many attempts to make exhibition-style qualified rides. One of the horses used for the impromptu bucking contest was a white-faced Bay named *Cyclone*. He was a good bucking horse to learn on, as he would stop bucking the moment he threw his rider. Pete was growing more competent in his bucking technique, his every move observed by the boys from the surrounding area who had arrived to watch the show, perched on the top rail of a corral and cheering the action on. Amongst these wide-eyed youngsters was Theodore Togstead – known to his friends as 'Teddy' – who would clearly remember, many years later, the place and time where Pete Knight began his legendary riding career. On those long, lazy Sunday afternoons, Pete rode as many as a dozen horses to the cheers, applause, and ribald remarks of his peers and neighbors.

With the war having taken many of the best riders from the district, Pete's chances of success at his first rodeo were considerably increased. Even with this in his favor, Pete was locally renowned as an exceptionally competent bronc rider in his own right. Riding to Crossfield, he paid his entry fee to the bucking event, and rode against competitors from across southern Alberta.

When the Crossfield Rodeo ended on a sunny afternoon in June, 1918, *The Chronicle* listed Pete Knight as a second-place winner of the bucking horse competition, the first official record of his participation in a bronc riding event.

As Pete was mounting his saddle pony to ride home from Crossfield with his winnings that day, the horse bolted across a field crowded with spectators and proceeded to buck its way into a three-strand barbed wire fence, causing both rider and horse to go down in a coiled mess of tangled wire. As bystanders pulled Pete away from the wreck (who was shaken but uninjured), and extricated the horse's hooves from the last strand of wire, the town constable threatened to cite the young man for hazardous conduct on bucking stock outside of a corral.

"He's no bronc," Pete replied. His reputation for honesty preceded him, in spite of his youth. "He's my riding pony."

With that explanation hanging in the air, the disgruntled constable ordered the young man to get on his horse and ride on out of town without further delay. Pete mounted up with hundreds of spectators watching his departure. With the horse kicking and bucking in spite of its injuries, rider and pony made their way over the distant horizon, Pete staying astride the horse the entire way.

Winning prize money in competition for the first time prompted Pete to raise a string of his own bucking horses; sturdy stock he also used to work the farm. Good bucking horses were not always in abundance at a small-town rodeo.

Pete's broncs could be entered in any rodeo, and would gain additional income for him beneath other riders, if horse and competing rider scored high points in the contest. By raising his own string of broncs, Pete also became one of Alberta's early 'rodeo stock' contractors. The best remembered of Pete's bucking horses was a big bay mare he named *Wampus Maude*. When the horse began tossing her head while pulling a one-way plow across a half-cultivated field, Pete could see in an instant that the restless horse needed a change of pace from the chore of plowing. Releasing Maude from her harness, he threw a saddle on her back, buckled on the spurs he kept under his plow-seat and swung aboard the leaping mount. The horse whirled and kicked across a half-plowed field in a bucking frenzy, until she had her fill of rider and spurs. Afterward, with Maude before the plow and Pete following with traces in hand, the business of pulling equipment in-harness would continue for the rest of the day.

Another noteworthy bronc in this string of amateur bucking horses was a mare Pete named *Sunfish Sadie* – not a difficult horse to ride but certainly one that looked good when she was bucking and twisting across an infield with a cowboy hanging onto her buck-rein.

Through Autumn of that year and into the Spring of the next, Pete entered in the saddle bronc bucking events at shows that included Elkton, Wetaskiwin, the Sunnyslope Stampede, and the Chestermere Lake Rodeo. Pete was making a name for himself in local rodeo circles, but the bucking horses at the small rodeos, the ability of the competition, and the amount of the prize-money being offered were all limited. Pete had become a strong rider, and was growing more formidable each day. The time had come to begin expanding his horizons, and hone his skills against better riders, on tougher horses.

As the war ended and the returned men from overseas came home to western Canada, a Victory Stampede was planned in Calgary to honor the winning of the conflict, in part by Canada's cowboys. The 1919 Stampede, only the second since the inception of the Calgary Stampede in 1912, paid tribute to the sacrifice of more than sixty-six thousand Canadian war dead and the hundreds of thousands of casualties who had returned to the Canadian west.

Clem Gardner, a locally renowned rancher from the Pirmez Creek-Jumping Pound range west of Calgary, entered as one of the favored contestants in the saddle bronc bucking competition. Another contender for the bucking horse championship was a young cowboy named 'Yakima' Cannutt, from Washington state. Cannutt would later become famous as the Hollywood stunt rider who taught legendary actor John Wayne to ride. Yakima performed many of the complicated and dangerous mounted scenes in big-budget classic movies of the 1930's and 40's, particularly in John Ford's "Rio Grande" and the epic production of "Stagecoach." Both films would cast John Wayne as the star performer. Pete, who was sixteen-years-old at the time Cannutt entered the Calgary Stampede, and a few years too young to compete in the stampede, attended each day of the riding events, hanging around behind the infield chutes. Standing shoulder-to-shoulder with the cowboys he idolized on the infield grounds, Pete made himself useful wherever he could as each contestant came charging out of a numbered chute on the back of a horse the rider had drawn.

Cannutt was one of Pete's all-time greatest heroes. Other riders would later claim they had heard Pete acknowledge Cannutt as the greatest bronc rider ever born. Pete had a front-row seat on the top rail of the chutes as he watched every move his hero made, his skin tingling as he observed Cannutt's style of spurring while the bronc bolted across the infield in a bucking frenzy.

When Cannutt was separated from his Stetson in a flurry of horse's mane, groaning saddle leather, and thundering hooves, Pete dashed out onto the infield at the end of the ride and retrieved his hero's hat. Like every young man who dreams of meeting a boy-hood idol, Pete was thrilled beyond speech after he introduced himself to Cannutt, who thanked him for recovering his Stetson. For a short time, Pete and Cannutt had an opportunity to get acquainted. Pete walked away a bigger Yakima-fan than he already had been.

In subsequent competition rides of his own, Pete copied Yakima's spurring style, but soon began to develop a style of his own that was distinct and unique. As he entered the bucking contests in Wetaskiwin, Carstairs, Cheadle, and on Clem Gardner's home ground at the Jumping Pound Rodeo, it was becoming evident that Pete Knight was a name to be reckoned with and his riding style was becoming smoother as the months progressed.

By the early 1920's, Pete's brothers and sisters had married and moved away from the family farm maintained by William and Katherine. Maggie married a Thatcher and moved to Beisecker, and Nellie married John McClain, who farmed east of Airdrie. Robert and Anna Knight had purchased their farm near Kersey and began a general trucking firm, while Walt and his wife Marie were then farming their own property in the same district. Pete remained the last son left to manage William's holdings.

At harvest time, Pete pitched bundles and scooped grain by hand, without mechanical assistance other than a large, flat, steel scoop-shovel. The hard work involved in the daily operation of an Alberta farm in those early years was one of the mitigating factors for Pete developing a pair of arms and shoulders that were muscular beyond average proportion. The aroma of freshly-gleaned grain wafted from the wagons and across the fields, while steam-driven tractors filled the air with black smoke. Steam engines drove the wheels of stationary, belt-driven threshing machines, as gangs made up of a dozen men fed the grain-stooks into one end, to winnow the barley, and collect the harvest from the other end. For Pete, each harvest-time on the prairies meant scooping grain, and driving mule-drawn wagons to the elevators, as greens turned to gold, and the autumn frosts began to harden in the coulees.

When the young man was finished his work at the end of each day, one of his favorite sports was running coyotes to ground. Coyotes were the bane of calves on the open range, and a small pack of coyotes could often be found stalking herds in search of food on the hoof. Racing a barely-trained saddle pony across a coulee or galloping across the length of a long ridge, Pete was often observed many miles from home, playing out a lariat and roping a lone coyote his horse had lit out after. While Pete was riding on range not yet completely fenced off, any stray horses that he came across – appearing to have no owner – he'd catch them up, rope, and deliver them on the hoof to the Deep Dale Ranch stock pound, to be sold at auction or driven home. Being William's son, Pete's curiosities were as instinctive as his father's. On one such occasion, Pete encountered a young moose in one of the coulees near his home, and roped the animal – leading him home with the intent of saddling and riding him. The moment Pete's back was turned, however, his moose sailed out of the Knight corral, clean over an eight-foot railing, while Pete was still dragging the saddle off his pony.

As the hard but colorful days of early Alberta range-life passed, Pete continued entering the local bucking competitions and always managed to win money at these amateur affairs. At the Crossfield Stampede from 1920, through to 1922, Pete won a small sum of money each year. He continued to compete at several of the small, local stampedes in Sunnyslope, Cheadle, and Water Valley.

It appeared that Pete was as ready as he would ever be, when he was invited by none other than Guy Weadick himself, to enter the Calgary Bucking Horse Contest. From his informal beginnings in the Deep Dale Ranch bucking corral, Pete was now heading for 'the big time.'

3
Breaking Into the Big Time

The American cowboy-performer, Guy Weadick, brought the idea of 'The Stampede' to Calgary during a 1904 horse-buying trip to what was then the Northwest Territories. Weadick – originally from Rochester, New York – fulfilled a lifelong dream to become a cowboy-performer, signing on as a trick-roper in vaudeville shows travelling across North America during the first decade of the twentieth century.

Convinced that Calgary would be an opportune centre to create a well-advertised tribute or 'Stampede,' to the old-timers and cowboys of the west, Weadick returned to southern Alberta in 1912 and solicited the assistance of Canadian Pacific Railway livestock agent, H.C. McMullen, who began a campaign to raise funds for the creation of a stampede.

The financial backing for the first stampede eventually came from four Calgary businessmen who would become famous as 'The Big Four' – George Lane, owner of the Bar U Ranch; Pat Burns, the meat-packing baron; gentleman-rancher and future Senator, A.E. Alfred 'Ernest' Cross, owner of southern Alberta's A7 Ranch; and Archie.J. MacLean, Alberta's Provincial Secretary. These four contributors accepted the risks involved and covered the cost of the first Calgary Stampede, held in September, 1912. Weadick was able to convince the Big Four that with their combined one hundred thousand dollar contribution, the prize-moneys awarded would be four times that of any comparable contest on the continent, that native involvement in the stampede's opening-day parade would be in the thousands, and that top bucking stock by the hundreds of head, would be made available from ranches across southern Alberta.

The first Calgary Stampede was unequivocally a great success, and figuratively became a feather in the city of Calgary's cap, for years after. However, the successful conclusion of the first stampede did not provide an assurance that the stampede would automatically become an annual event. Eleven years after the Big Four's initial involvement, the Calgary Stampede of 1923 was only the third time the contest had ever been planned; the stampede would become an annual event after that summer, and it was to that year's contest that Pete Knight first entered his name in the bucking horse event.

It wasn't often that a barely-known young man from the prairies received the stampede manager's personal invitation to compete in the greatest bronc riding competition in Canada. Pete was barely twenty years of age, and had gained considerable recognition as an up-and-coming bronc rider.

The 1923 Calgary Stampede would also receive a form of royal assent, as well as royal patronage from an unexpected source. The Prince of Wales, who was heir to the British throne and destined to become King Edward VIII, visited Calgary in 1919 and came away greatly impressed with western Canada. So taken was this royal son by the grandeur and beauty of Alberta that the Prince purchased a ranch near Longview, Alberta, and registered a cattle-brand with the initials denoting his name and station, as 'Edward Prince.' The Prince of Wales Ranch came to be known affectionately to cowboys on the eastern slopes of the Rocky Mountains as the 'EP.' Its ranges bordered two of the most famous ranches in southern Alberta; the 'OH' and the 'Bar U,' making the Prince's ranch easy to locate. The cowboy spirit that the Prince of Wales found in Alberta's foothills carried its own unwritten code of respect and chivalry, and a simple gesture or turn of phrase from a lone cowboy at work would speak volumes about his integrity and way of life.

As a sign of his genuine affection for the cowboys surrounding his new 'home away from London Palaces' on the majestic, sweeping vistas of Alberta's foothills, the future King dedicated a new and distinguished silver trophy, 'The Prince of Wales Cup,' to be awarded to the top Canadian Bucking Horse rider. The cup was designed by the Royal Jewelers in London, England, and was completed in time for the Awards Ceremony at the 1923 Calgary Stampede. For a contestant to qualify for the Prince of Wales Cup, the cowboy had to be a Canadian and had to make his permanent home in Canada. The cowboy competitor who met these qualifications also had to win the Canadian Bucking Championship at the Calgary Stampede in order to have his name placed on the trophy. As an added consolation, the contestant who won the championship on three occasions and not necessarily in three consecutive years, would keep the solid-silver cup as his personal property.

Physically and figuratively, the Prince of Wales Cup carried greater prestige in its era than any other trophy ever awarded in a Canadian sporting event, even against those cups and trophies presented for hockey or football competition. Standing almost three feet tall and tooled in gleaming silver on a hardwood plinth, the Prince of Wales Cup drove bucking horse riding competition to a new and interesting height. Any cowboy of any riding ability found anywhere in western Canada was determined to make his way to Calgary to compete for the Prince's Cup. As a cowboy with more than respectable riding ability, Pete saw the chance to ride for the Prince of Wales Cup as additional challenging incentive to what was already a weekly pastime for most of the young men he knew.

Pete enjoyed being a grain farmer like his father and older brothers , but he also had a great love for riding, caring for, and competing on horses. The camaraderie and wild, death-defying excitement found at the local stampedes filled Pete with a dream of fulfilling a life-long ambition: to be a champion bucking horse rider. Guy Weadick's invitation to Pete, after Weadick had witnessed the young rider's incredible strength, balance, and skill on bucking horses at a dozen small stampedes across southern Alberta, was confirmation of what Pete already suspected in his heart. The rodeo would dominate his life, and he in turn, would dominate the rodeo.

The Calgary Stampede parade was similar to the parades that marked the official beginning of the International Olympic Games as they have been in recent years. The contestants were expected by the stampede's organizers to participate in the parade or 'Grand Entry,' as some stampede organizers called it. Decked out in full western regalia, the cowboys who rode down Calgary's Ninth Avenue in the Stampede parade wore chaps, spurs, tall-top western boots, and the ever-popular Stetsons. Their contestant numbers, pinned to the backs of their gaudy silk shirts, flapped in the morning breeze as they rode their ponies down Calgary's spectator-packed avenues.

Riders from across the continent had travelled to Calgary, to take their places in the greatest western competition ever held, and the Grand Entry was their rite of passage. From old hands of the big-city vaudeville and rodeo circuits, to new entrants such as Pete – who had never before entered as prestigious a stampede as this one – all stampede competitors and parade entries were treated to the same rousing applause, thunderous cheering, and other expressions of appreciation and admiration from tens of thousands of spectators. They came to Calgary in droves from across North America, and even as far away as Europe and Australia. Pete Knight would forever be affected by the accolades he shared with his fellow competitors in that first Calgary Stampede parade, never dreaming at the time that his star would rise far beyond that of his boyhood hero, Yakima Cannutt.

While the Monday morning pageant progressed, the crowd lining the route spared no expense in their applause and cheering, expressions of appreciation on a scale that Pete had never before experienced. The fans pressed out onto the avenue past the curbs and gutters, clapping and waving hats and sharing in the revelry. The horses and their riders, three and four abreast, rode by the cheering spectators in column after column on city pavement made slick with the pungent defecation of thousands of mules and horses, and the constant washing down from the city's water-works. Cowboys rode on with their hats in their free hands, standing in their stirrups and belting out whoops and yodels in response to the cheering of the crowd.

As the column of contestants rode by the Palliser Hotel and neared the CPR Station at Centre Street, a marching band struck up a popular tune with a crash of cymbals and spooked Pete's horse. Caught up with the excitement of thousands of people hollering and clapping, the nervous, fidgety pony became increasingly skittish, hard to handle, and began to buck. Hooves went skidding from beneath the horse, pitching both rider and mount onto the wet pavement in an audible heap of breaking bone and shouted agony.

The horse was fine and quickly regained his footing, but Pete had a badly broken left leg that demanded immediate attention at Calgary's General Hospital. For the rest of the summer and most of that autumn Pete was physically laid up at the farm, where his leg remained in a plaster cast until Christmas of 1923. With both of his parents aging and unwell, Pete had the grim task of hobbling from house to barn and back and completing his daily chores as best he could, while his parents questioned the value of his involvement in such a rough sport, especially with so little gain to show for the effort.

Like his father and grandfather before him, once Pete set his mind to achieving a goal, he allowed nothing to stand in his way. Pete began to work the muscles of his long-immobilized leg, engaging in any farm chore that would increase his strength, leaving him bathed in perspiration but with a strong sense of satisfaction for the effort expended. The horse falling on his leg had been an unforeseen setback that he was determined to overcome.

Through the spring of 1924, Pete began to ride again, although the leg he had fractured would continue to plague his competitive riding ability for the rest of his career, causing him to 'lose a stirrup' at a critical moment, in the years ahead. By late spring he was again competing in a long list of small southern Alberta rodeos, winning money at Crossfield and at Chestermere Lake Stampede against a growing list of outstanding riders, all of whom eagerly discussed the Prince's Cup.

Midnight was a professionally-untried bucking horse, and his owner, Jim McNab, of Fort MacLeod, believed the horse would be an acceptable addition to any rodeo's bucking stock. This tall black gelding, sired by a Percheron-Morgan cross on the Cottonwood Ranch in southern Alberta's Porcupine Hills, was eight-years-old when he was entered at Macleod Rodeo. *Midnight* had initially been saddle-broke at three years of age, however, his temperament became completely unpredictable. His owner finally decided the horse could never be used as a saddle horse, and began to enter *Midnight* at several of the local rodeos in the Macleod area. Pete Bruisedhead, an Indian rider from Alberta's Blood Reserve at Standoff, was one of the first documented contestants ever to make a clean competition ride on *Midnight*, at Fort Macleod, in the first week of July 1924. The horse was shipped with other stock to Calgary for the following week's bucking event. At the Calgary Stampede and forever after, this horse would become a legendary bucking phenomenon and the subject of song and myth – and in the course of *Midnight's* life, few cowboy contestants would ever ride this huge black bronc to a successful conclusion. Before the famous bucking horse and the future bronc riding legend would first lay eyes upon each other, however, contests of lesser importance for both of them would intervene.

The second annual Carstairs Stampede was held at the railroad loading chutes of the small Alberta town on Saturday, July 5, 1924, and the one-day affair featured a host of well-known southern Alberta cowboys who gave a paying crowd of thousands an afternoon performance worthy of the greatest stampede. The winner in the bucking event at Carstairs was 'Slim' Watrin, of High River, Alberta. The oldest three of four Watrin Brothers – Slim, Eddie, and Leo – were renowned across the province for their riding ability and often left the infields of Alberta's small stampedes with the prize money or the second, third, or fourth-place winnings in the bucking competition. Pete knew he was up against the toughest competitors to be found anywhere in rodeo competition.

Pete Knight drew a horse named *Grey Ghost* at this event and was making a spectacular ride when he was thrown without injury, thirty yards from the chutes. Although Pete made no money from his own riding performance that day, two of his personal string of contracted bucking horses, *Wampus Ribbon* and *Lightning Rod*, were among the best buckers of the afternoon and won second and third-place prize money for the riders who had drawn them, with a percentage being paid to Pete.

The Carstairs Stampede drew to a close, and Pete once again mounted his saddle horse, his bucking horses haltered and strung out behind on a lead line, their glossy brown hides rippling as they cantered along behind their owner. He rode eastward at a brisk pace – over twenty miles of rolling range and gently-sloping farmland – toward his parent's home, across the Rosebud River. As Pete rode on, his passing startled a herd of mule deer, and flocks of mallard ducks took flight off of the water's surface, as his horses splashed across the river on the trek toward home. It was a more tranquil world he rode through than the exciting one he'd just left behind. He was looking forward to a few days of rest that would serve him well, before entering the bucking horse contest the following week in Calgary.

The 1924 Calgary Stampede began on Monday, July 7, with the stampede parade opening the festivities at 10:00 a.m. that morning. The theme of that year's stampede was billed "Bigger and Better," and the stampede's participants along with the citizens of Calgary, were determined to make that a reality. The money being offered in cash and prizes in the contest events exceeded fifty-five thousand dollars, and was the main subject of discussion for cowboys across North America.

The parade featured one thousand mounted riders, hundreds of Indians in full regalia, and a march past of the last surviving veterans of the Northwest Mounted Police members who had first arrived in the 'lawless' Northwest Territories. Red River carts and chuck-wagons rolled along the parade route, and biplanes from the Air Force's High River station buzzed overhead. A wagon train consisting of eight attached grain wagons driven by 'Slim' Moorehouse of Gleichen, Alberta, and pulled by twenty-two horses and ten mules, thundered down the streets of Calgary with that solitary driver at the reins. Moorehouse enjoyed the reputation in the city of being a prank-pulling exhibitionist of rare quality.

In a mishap similar to Pete Knight's from the previous year, a young cowboy who gave his address as "East Second Street, Calgary," sustained a fractured ankle when his horse slipped in the parade and fell with his rider beneath him. Feats of tough-guy derring-do at Calgary's Palace Theatre were featured in movies such as "The Boy of Flanders," while silver screen Cowboy 'Hoot' Gibson starred at the Regent Theatre in "Ride For Your Life." The famous cowboy's name served as a marquee backdrop to the spectacle of each passing parade entry. More than two hundred private automobiles carrying tourists to Calgary, registered at the St. Patrick's Island Auto Camp, and every hotel room in the city was filled to capacity. In the setting of a city appearing to have gone completely 'wild western,' the stampede's infield events began that Monday afternoon.

In the bucking horse competition, the preliminary rides were divided between Monday and Tuesday for the dozens of riders competing in this premier event. On Tuesday, July 8, Pete Knight qualified in second place behind Pete La Grandeur of Pincher Creek, Alberta, before a crowd of more than twenty-six thousand spectators. The two Alberta cowboys had ridden in the eliminations against a veritable 'who's who' of top-notch bronc riders from across the west. Pete Knight was confident of his ability, but several times came close to losing a stirrup – a legacy from his previous year's ankle fracture. The names of the rankest broncs he had ever seen were being drawn from the hat, and as a matter of course, were taking their toll against exceptional riders. As the week's program progressed, the cowboys who were eliminated from the competition and had won consolation prizes for their rides that week, could fill a volume of Canadian Rodeo-history's Star Performers.

Bert Shepard of High River, Pete Bruisedhead of Standoff, Charlie McDonald of Calgary and many more outstanding riders had been knocked out of the contest by a ferocious herd of notable horses, as well as by younger, more agile and luckier riders. By Thursday night, the competition was narrowed to five cowboys who would make semi-final rides on the following Friday. Two Americans, Scott Seeley and Cecil Henley, were up against Canadian boys Bayse Collins of Elnora, Alberta, Pete La Grandeur and newcomer Pete Knight. Cecil Henley, from Washington state, drew *Midnight* for his Friday competition ride, and after three short jumps, the horse piled Henley into the infield dust, while Bayse Collins rode *Tumbleweed* to a third place finish. Pete Knight had drawn *Alberta Kid*, a horse that was rated as the toughest bucking bronc at the previous year's Calgary Stampede; the same horse that Alberta cowboy Pete Vandermeer had ridden to a successful and winning completion in the 1923 competition for the Prince of Wales Cup. *Alberta Kid* had the dubious reputation of being a 'bad horse extraordinaire,' and the ride that Pete Knight performed on the back of this wild, highly-regarded bucking horse, before a crowd of over twenty-thousand spectators that afternoon, would be talked about for more than half a century.

As Pete Knight passed the plane of the chute on *Alberta Kid*, the horse let out a scream, plunged straight up into the air and came back down in a bone-jarring shock of hooves, slamming onto the infield and taking the collective breath away from thousands of spectators. The horse twisted to his left, all the while leaping skyward and returning to earth with his hind-hooves flailing in the air. With grim determination, Pete gripped the buck-rein in one clenched fist, maintaining his hold and his balance on the wildly-churning horse. The ten-second gun fired to mark a successful ride, as the judges nodded their satisfaction and began to add up

The Bronc Riding Finalists, Calgary Stampede, 1924
Pete Le Grandeur of Pincher Creek, Alberta won the Canadian Bucking Championship while Pete Knight took second place with less than a one point difference between the two scores.
From left to right: Pete Seely, Cecil Henley, Pete Le Grandeur, Bayse Collins, Pete Knight.
Photo source: Author

the points Pete had accrued. Stampede Manager Guy Weadick was watching the ride from behind the infield chutes, and nodded his approval of Pete's battle with *Alberta Kid*, while his chute foreman and a half dozen other riders nearby shook their heads in disbelief – they in turn, acknowledging the near-impossibility of anyone remaining aboard this ferocious bucking horse. At that moment, it appeared that Pete Knight would win the national championship.

Pete La Grandeur drew a horse named *Yellow Fever*, and made an excellent, well-balanced ride on this bucking ferocity, but did not stir the crowd as Pete Knight had on *Alberta Kid*. The points that La Grandeur had accumulated during his preliminary ride on the previous Tuesday, however – on a horse named *Sky Blue* – solidly placed the Pincher Creek cowboy as the winner of the Canadian Bucking Horse Championship for 1924, by the narrow margin of less than one-tenth of a point ahead of Pete Knight.

The two Pete's were called before the Grandstand together to receive the appreciation of the crowd, as thousands of spectators took to their feet and cheered the two Alberta cowboys in a frenzy of applause. Stampede Chairman A. 'Ernest' Cross, accompanied by Manager Guy Weadick, were both on hand to congratulate the winners and present each cowboy with his deserving award.

To the astonishment and collective awe of all who knew him in the Crossfield district, Pete Knight, the polite, quiet young man from the Wigle farm – that wild young boy who would take on any horse he encountered and attempt to ride the brute to a stand-still – was elevated upon his own merit and riding ability to the position of runner-up to the top bucking horse rider in Canada. From that day on, fame for Pete Knight would be enduring.

4

A Winning Reputation

Fame, admiration from his peers, and seeing his name often repeated in the newspapers didn't change Pete Knight, and he didn't let these accolades go to his head. Pete remained the well-liked, pleasant young man he had been raised to be. With the winning of the second-place position behind La Grandeur, Pete joined in the celebrations held for his near-victory, but brimmed with a quiet confidence, as he speculated to himself about his hopes for the future in rodeo.

As the summer of 1924 turned to autumn, harvest-time descended on the southern Alberta prairie, and Pete's efforts focused on the hitching of teams of dray horses to grain wagons, and the cutting, threshing and hauling of that year's crop. Sundays were supposed to be days of rest and leisure, but the boys would inevitably saddle up their horses and ride over to the Deep Dale Ranch, to compete against each other on Togstead's best bucking horses, before the winter set in. When the first snowflakes fell on the cold, wind-swept plain, the boys hung up their buck-reins until the following April.

As the final days of winter made way for the spring of 1925, the last of the winter snow melted from the drab brown prairie and the rodeos of southern Alberta once again began their annual cycle.

The Crossfield Stampede was a two-day event, and keen competition was a hallmark for that year's rodeo. The citizens of this small Alberta town had spent several months rebuilding two whole blocks of the town's core businesses, after two devastating fires had ripped through town's centre in the previous year. Alberta's motto could have been an unwritten command to build, grow, and grow bigger. The new Oliver Hotel boasted eighteen bedrooms with hot and cold running water, over-sized cast iron bathtubs on each floor, and a restaurant that served the finest cuts of grade-A Alberta beef. Just as Pete broken leg had not deterred his ambition, neither did his home town's spirit break when the destruction of a fire came sweeping through its midst. Crossfield's business-owners, and the town's community-minded citizens, often boasted of having had their 'home town boy' win second place in the national bucking championship. On days when Pete rode into town for his family's provisions, the renowned young bronc rider could always be found at the Crossfield men's-wear store or at the local saddler, quietly chatting the hours away with the proprietor and a host of good friends and admirers. The town's enthusiasm for bucking horse competition was fueled by their local champion's success, and Crossfield's citizens bore a deep pride in having Pete living amongst them.

Pete Knight won the day money in the Thursday, July 2, Crossfield Stampede bucking event, with his strong lead followed by Slim Watrin of High River. Third place went to an up-and-coming young cowboy from Cochrane, Walter Armsdon. The three riders finished in those positions on the following day, for the titles and awards they carried away from the rodeo.

Heavy rain fell to herald the 1925 Calgary Stampede, in the week following Pete's success at Crossfield, but the drizzle did not dampen the spirits of the revelers who came out to watch and participate in the Stampede parade on that wet July Monday morning. Slim Moorehouse of Gleichen was once again featured driving his famous teams of thirty-six all-black Belgian dray-horses. With harness rings jingling and leather traces slapping their cadence, the powerful assemblage pulled ten hitched wagons loaded to the brims with Marquis wheat. Marching bands played, Indians by the hundreds rode in costume, and the crowds cheered. The Midway at the Exhibition grounds featured the Rubin & Cherry travelling shows, with their merry-go-round horses and a huge Ferris-wheel. A top-quality Stetson could be purchased in Calgary for five dollars; a new Dodge Brothers Automobile for a thousand. The British Field Marshall, Earl Haig, – who had commanded Canada's soldiers on the European battlefields of the recent world war – was accompanied by thirty staff aides, servants and junior officers, as the General's entourage arrived at Calgary's CPR Station that week. The Field Marshall was accorded the highest honors by the stampede's management and other local officials, and Haig would in turn preside over the stampede's competitive events. Pete Knight travelled to Calgary by passenger rail-car, leaving his bucking horses on the farm and his saddlepony at a stable near the Crossfield train station.

In the week's bucking horse competition, the list of contestants who were favored to win high points – including Pete Vandermeer, Slim Watrin, Pete La Grandeur, Bayse Collins, and Pete Knight – did not ride to the expectations of the grandstand crowd. Although Vandermeer and La Grandeur had won top honors in previous years at the stampede, other riders of lesser local fame achieved the highest scores, much to everyone's collective surprise.

Pete Knight initially qualified during the Monday elimination rides on a horse name *Highland Fling,* placing the young rider in third place position behind two American cowboys, 'Breezy' Cox of Arizona, and Cecil Henley of

Photo source: *Glenbow Archives*

Washington state. On the Friday following, with the competition narrowed down to forty-four riders, Pete drew the horse named *Grey Ghost.* This was a horse that had thrown him in Carstairs the year before. The big-boned, tall grey bronc leaped into the infield in a high arc and came down in a pitching, kicking swirl of dust. On the second jump, Pete lost his Stetson and a stirrup – his old ankle injury once again affecting his performance – before the ten-second gun was fired, automatically disqualifying him. Breezy thrilled the crowd with a spectacular ride on a horse called *Twenty Seven Bucks,* winning the North American Bucking championship. Al Falconer of Cardston, Alberta, won the runner-up position and the Prince of Wales Cup on *Cheadle Lass,* a horse of hard-bucking reputation. Pete Vandermeer, Pete La Grandeur, Fred Hunt and Bayse Collins all failed to qualify, while Leo Watrin took the two hundred-fifty dollar prize offered to the third-place winner, followed by Sykes Robinson of Cochrane, Alberta, in fourth position. Another stampede had concluded and already the contestants were looking to the next show.

To cover more ground to rodeos held farther afield, Pete purchased a used Model-T Ford, and began travelling with other cowboys to distant stampedes across Alberta. Where Pete had previously been able to ride on horse-back at his leisure to local rodeos with his bucking horses on a lead line, he soon became adept at travelling quickly to more distant and bigger stampedes, winning the bucking horse event, and continuing on to the next town featuring a stampede. He often drove into the wee hours of an early morning at break-neck speeds on primitive highways that had little or no patrol and few late-night services. His brother Walt often accompanied Pete on the 'rodeo circuit.' They'd take a hotel room in the town hosting the contest, or take turns at the wheel while the other brother slept. It was often the case that the car was filled with other contestants along for the ride.

Prior to the summer of 1925, Walt's two infant sons, Harry and Tom, died one after the other of pneumonia and were buried at the family farm. The loss of the two boys was a blow to the entire family. Life on the farm carried on, and Walt and Marie continued to persevere. Although Pete was nearly sixteen years younger than Walt, he helped his older brother get over the loss, encouraging him to come on the road with him during rodeo season.

With Marie remaining at their farm-home with other relatives to help out, Walt travelled the circuit with Pete. It was common for men to leave everyone and everything behind at home in the 1920's to travel in pursuit of business. The two brothers kept each other company on the road to distant competitions, building an unshakable camaraderie.

There was little that Pete had to have with him, in the trunk of his Model-T. His saddle, spurs, buck-rein, and a change of clothing were all he needed. With enough cash in his wallet to pay the entry fee and cover his expenses, he was practically set. This, after all, was as much a business as any other, and the rodeo business was good in the 1920's, for tough young men who had ability, talent and weren't easily swayed by the bottle. The desire to move quickly and travel light was a family trait that had been passed down from William to his sons.

In a stampede event that involved a crew of men or teams of horses and a wagon or favored roping horses and lariats, Pete Knight was as competent at driving teams of horses as professionals Tom Lauder or Dick Cosgrave – the acknowledged experts of the chuck-wagon races of the 1920's – and was as agile and accurate with a lariat as the leading calf-ropers of his day. These, however, were not 'his events,' and consequently, he would not typically be billed as an 'All-Around Cowboy.' That, however, did not bother Pete. He specialized in the saddle bronc bucking event, and focused his energies on the thrill of competition and the winnings he could make in that one event. He was a bronc rider of extraordinary finesse, with the physical strength to match.

Newspaper articles written on Alberta's early rodeos made fleeting mention that Pete Knight had participated in the wild horse race event at a particular small-town stampede here or there. The race was similar in some aspects to the bucking horse event, with saddle. The contestant guided his wild, saddled bucking horse on a specified course, and hung onto the horse as he rode. The cowboy who partici-pated in this event also had two other contestants on his team, and the horse they caught was roped at random from a herd while other teams of contestants were attempting the same feat. After successfully catching their horse, two of the con-testants saddled the unbroken pony in the open while the third man, the 'ear downer,' bit into the horse's ear as he held the horse around the neck, thereby calming the shaking animal long enough to be saddled without kicking the three men to death. The ear-downer's distasteful job would never change through the decades to follow. The horse was hastily bridled and the best rider of the three mounted up. The ear-downer released the horse's head and the rider would then buck his mount in the direction predetermined by the contest rules. Everyone knew Pete's first ambition was in the bucking horse event. That, after all, was the true 'lone knight' occupation of the stampede – the premier event of every rodeo in North America – and Pete's first love. It involved the greatest individual danger but reaped the biggest rewards for the sole contestant, where one expert rider placed all of his skill against one superbly notorious bucking horse, fully saddled and quickly released. Charging from an infield chute from 'stand-still' – in a fight for supremacy that carried the bronc rider through a nightmarish ten seconds – both horse or contestant could be battered, bloodied . . . or killed. Bronc riders los-ing their place in the saddle – an upset to their delicate balance and timing with boots spurring in stirrups and buck-rein 'see-sawing' in a clenched fist – were often thrown through solid wooden railings or wire fences. Horses bucked in a maddened frenzy over high walls and through chute gates and onto the bleacher seating of stampede grandstands, rupturing themselves and often crushing their riders in the process. It was a blood-sport born of the plains, but an honest depiction of the daily life faced by the last western hero – the cowboy – on a frontier that was rapidly vanishing.

Pete was a bronc rider with exceptional focus, and all else was either too slow or too tedious for his temperament. This is not to say that he was not a team play-er, for indeed he was. Pete was often called upon to stand in as the undeclared cap-tain of the team in times of crisis. It was a consequence of his nature. He took care of other contestants when the chips were down for those riders who were injured or left penniless as a result of a stampede competition. In an era where social secu-rity, workmen's compensation or cowboy contestant insurance were unheard of, cowboys took it upon themselves to look out for each other. The stronger always took up the slack for the weaker; a strong sense of moral duty ever guiding the actions of those able to help. Dignity remained one of the shining attributes in a cowboy's unwritten code of conduct, and that dignity was protected in turn by the winners of bronc-riding competition, who would fork out the needed cash to pay for a fellow-competitor's hospital bills, food, or entry fee to the next rodeo. At the forefront of these quiet contributors – many shelling out huge sums of cash to their less-fortunate brethren, and never expecting back or asking for a dime in return –was Pete Knight.

5

The Travelling Stampede

As the summer of 1925 fully bloomed in Alberta, all of the big-money stampedes in the province ended for the season. However, a bold plan had been in the making for many months to take a stampede on the road. This novel but not completely original idea was the brainchild of enterprising Calgary entrepreneur, Peter Welsh. Welsh, with his extensive experience in horse-show organization and who also owned a stable of show horses that included the great jumping horse *Bara Ladd*, incorporated *The Alberta Stampede Company*, preparing to take the show on the road in the first weeks of that summer. The Alberta Stampede Company was essentially a re-creation of the Wild West shows that had toured the United States and England during the last decade of the nineteenth century and the first few years of the 1900's. Unlike its predecessors, Welsh's show toured without the mounted 'trick shooters' or 'wild Indians' that had made men such as William 'Buffalo Bill' Cody so famous. To compensate for the lack of gun-toting pistoleros and Eagle-feather-clad natives, and to set his production apart from any other, Welsh had to recruit the top riders and the best bucking horses he could find to draw paying crowds in cities far from Alberta's ranching country. Pete Vandermeer, who had won the Canadian national bronc-riding championship in 1923, and the swarthy, mischievously-grinning Frank Sharp, who would soon become one of Canada's first bull-riding champions, were among the many Alberta riders invited to sign on with Welsh's company of international stars. On this list of reputable riders who would go on the road to ride in real rodeo contests for hundreds of thousands of spectators from British Columbia's lower mainland to the city of Montreal, Pete Knight's name was at the top. In addition to receiving travelling expenses, the cowboys would all compete in open rodeo competition, including the Saddle Bronc bucking event which featured prize-purses far in excess of any amount awarded to that date, in any of Alberta's major stampedes.

Peter Welsh and his flamboyant partner 'Strawberry Red' Woll – for the astounding price of five hundred dollars – purchased the legendary coal-black bucking horse, *Midnight*. More than a hundred other horses were needed to make the show a success, and Welsh made offers to every known horse-dealer in southern Alberta, in his search for bucking stock. From Joe Laycock of Okotoks, Alberta, Welsh purchased a notorious, scruffy little bronc who would become famous across the continent as *Five Minutes to Midnight*. 'Little Five,' as he was affectionately referred to by the cowboys who rode him, would, in time, throw the best riders that competition could offer. The price Welsh paid for *Five Minutes to Midnight* was never disclosed, but against the astounding purchase price paid for *Midnight,* speculation on *Little Five's* value ran rife.

In the week following the concluding ceremonies of the 1925 Calgary Stampede, Welsh's company produced the highly-acclaimed Edmonton Stampede, featuring the best riders and toughest bucking horses in the west. On the first day of the Edmonton show, the renowned Pete Vandermeer – tall, lanky, and often referred to by his many fans as The Prince of Wales Cowboy – was rushed from the infield to an Edmonton hospital after receiving a severe mauling from the horse he had drawn. Vandermeer had left the chute on one of Welsh's most savage buckers, and was quickly pummeled in a merciless onslaught against the infield rails. Knocked unconscious and bleeding from his ears and nose, The Prince of Wales Cowboy was carried away, as a hush descended throughout the grandstand. The stampede was not being 'staged,' simply as a performance – this was 'the real McCoy' where the battle between horse and rider was being fought to a grim, bloodied finalé. By word of mouth alone, the number of spectators to the stampede's following-day performance swelled dramatically.

As the week drew on, a long list of Welsh's reputable contestants were either bucked off, or failed to accrue high points in the premier event; from stirrups lost or failing to spur the horse or from grabbing saddle-horns. A murmur began to circulate through the crowd that the horses were too tough for the cowboys. On the final afternoon, Pete Knight drew a horse named *Gravedigger*. A dark dappled roan and first-string bucking horse, *Gravedigger* was notorious – this horse had killed a bronc rider earlier that year at the Vernon Stampede in British Columbia's Okanagan Valley.

As the gate swung open, horse and rider passed the plane of chute, *Gravedigger* taking a great lunge into the air before coming down hard on his hooves. A long line of battered, scraped cowboys – one with an arm in a cast and sling – hovered on the top rail of the infield chutes as Pete passed beside and above them, *Gravedigger* swaying back and forth in a pendulum of lathered horse-hide and audibly-straining saddle leather. The crowd held its collective breath and anticipated another wreck – another rider to be carried off in need of a doctor's attention – from a high-flying bronc.

With his buck-rein clenched firmly in one hand, Pete matched the horse's every turn, the rider's spurs slashing the air in a visual cacophony of reflected silver, his chaps flailing against the bucking horse's shoulders and ribs. Pete rode the wildly-bucking *Gravedigger* across the stadium infield – his boots firmly in control of his stirrups, his style, poise, and balance impeccable – to a spectacular finalé and the rousing applause of Edmonton's sold-out crowd of spectators rising from their seats in the stands, and his fellow cowboys cheering him on from the chutes.

Welsh had ensured that his stampede would receive greater billing than the Calgary affair, and his promise of a larger purse to the winning contestants was kept. Pete received one thousand dollars in cash, a handsome hand-tooled saddle donated by an Edmonton outfitter, a championship belt, and a solid-gold buckle donated by Edmonton Exhibition Manager, Percy Abbott. The second-place winner was American rider, Jesse Coates from Jerome, Idaho, who had drawn a horse named *Baldy* and spurred the bronc to a close finish behind Pete. Another Idahoan, Frank Studnick, had drawn *Midnight* and barely managed to stay in the saddle. Studnick was unable to spur the great black gelding to the judges' satisfaction and lost many points in the contest, clenching the buck-rein for dear life while managing to make the best of his ride. Fourth place was captured by Leo Watrin on a horse named *Bassano Boy*, after the young rider catapulted from the chute in a twisting flurry of horse's mane and hooves. Leo, one of the four famous bronc riding Watrin brothers from High River, Alberta, was in his first year of professional competition, but already taking on 'greats' of the era such as Pete Knight, Frank Studnick, Alec La Framboise and Pete Forester, and riding against his own brothers.

His older brother, Slim, drew a horse of wicked bucking reputation named *Tumbleweed*, but when bronc and rider left the chute, the horse made only a half-hearted attempt to buck, leaving the rider short of qualifying points. With Pete Knight's outstanding ride on *Gravedigger* having concluded the contest, the points tallied from the competition left little to be said about Pete's ability, from the other cowboys. The summer, after all, was far from over, and cowboys are noted for their optimism. The 1925 stampede held in Alberta's capital city ended with the riders taking their winnings and moving on, as the company carried its horses and riders by rail-car to the next big city show.

Although the horse named *Midnight* and Crossfield's acclaimed champion rider had seen each other at the latest bucking event, Pete had yet to draw the big black gelding for a contest that was already being talked about by cowboys from

Pete Knight riding Gravedigger

The Alberta Stampede Company, in Vancouver, British Columbia, 1926.

Photo source: Harold Knight Collection

every corner of the west. The boys who had already ridden *Midnight* were in a world of their own, and discussion amongst the stampede's riders constantly turned to the jet black horse's ability to thwart a cowboy's efforts to stay in the saddle. As the discussion lengthened into verbal obsession – the object of their obsessive orations stood in his boxcar stall and obliviously chewed his hay, just four cars back. In the dining car, and later, in the Pullman car carrying the boys on steel rails to the next show, Pete paid rapt attention to the blow-by-blow recollections given from riders who had drawn *Midnight* and said little himself, itching for his chance to take on the big gelding. During the summer of 1925, *Midnight*, like his cowboy counterpart, was fortifying a reputation that would eventually span decades and generations.

The Alberta Stampede Company took its version of the wild west stampede contest across Canada; from Vancouver, British Columbia to Winnipeg, Manitoba; from Toronto and Ottawa in Ontario, to Montreal, Quebec. Later, the company would also feature stampede events in the American cities of Buffalo in up-state New York; Columbus, Ohio; and Detroit, Michigan, – performing before American crowds of considerably greater numbers than found at those shows featured in Canada's eastern cities. As the summer ended and Pete returned to Calgary with the stampede troupe, he reflected upon a year of successful competition and a legion of new friends he'd made across the breadth of the country.

With more money having been made in winnings and a newer automobile to carry him to the next rodeo, Pete returned to his parent's rented family farm after that year's stampede season and purchased a section of farmland for himself, two miles east of the Deep Dale Ranch. A local farmer and businessman named James, owner of the James Cartage Company was a friend of Pete's. James Cartage contracted to haul goods for farmers in the district, initially by mule-drawn wagon and later with freight trucks; he would later become a successful founding partner of James and Reimer Oilfield Trucking of Calgary. With this businessman's assistance, Pete was able to purchase his first and only land possession. From his itinerant bronc rider occupation, Pete's desire was to have a home of his own, where he could invest his yet-uncertain winnings, live close to his family and possibly put down roots of his own at a later date. His down-payment made and his ownership filed at the land titles office in Calgary, Pete prepared to take the crop off of his recently-acquired section of farmland.

In the spring of 1926, tragedy struck Pete's family with the sudden death of his sister-in-law Anna and her newborn baby daughter, while she visited relatives in Oklahoma. Several weeks after her sudden loss, Pete's mother Katherine passed away in her old age and was mourned by the Knight family and their many friends in the Crossfield district. Katherine, having journeyed far from her native Ireland, had seen her locally-famous son compete on an even footing against the best riders in North America. Despite her initial misgivings over her son's career choice, before she died, Katherine told Pete she was deeply proud of him. A huge black granite stone was placed in Katherine's memory over her grave in Crossfield's cemetery, which would retain its splendor into the following century. With the loss of loved ones and the passing of time, however, life continued for Pete and the rest of his family, and June was the beginning of stampede season in western Canada.

Calgary did not see Pete Knight in its bucking horse contest of 1926. In the week prior to the Calgary Stampede, the Alberta Stampede Company's riders were featured in a Dominion Day Stampede, a thousand miles to the east in Winnipeg, Manitoba. The stampede company's existence was viewed by Guy Weadick to be a conflict of interest with the Calgary Stampede, causing him to threaten Peter Welch with legal action, for using the word 'Stampede' in his show. However, nothing came of the lawsuit.

The Winnipeg event was billed as a 'World Championship' bucking horse contest. In many cases, the horses stole the show in defeating their riders, with *Midnight, Tumbleweed, High Tower,* and *Red Devil* all bucking cowboys off into the infield dirt. Pete had thrilled a crowd of twenty thousand spectators in the course of the week, with his riding prowess on six of Welsh's highly-notorious bucking horses – on some days, riding one bronc minutes after leaving the back of another.

By overwhelming acclaim and with a point-score far ahead of the nearest competitor, Pete was declared winner of the show's 'North American Open' bucking event. He was presented with a fifteen hundred dollar cash prize, a hand-built saddle donated by Winnipeg's 'E.F. Hutchings' firm, and a silver-mounted bridle donated by Hollywood's foremost 'silver screen' cowboy star, Tom Mix. Phyllis Webb, the daughter of Winnipeg Mayor Ralph Webb, made the presentations to the cowboys, while an enthusiastic crowd cheered the proceedings. In a gesture brimming with good sportsmanship, Pete relinquished claim of the saddle and bridle he had just won to young Oliver Mott, a twenty-year-old cowboy from Kamloops, British Columbia. The young British Columbian achieved first place in the show's 'Canadian Bucking' event that afternoon, to the collective delight of a crowd highly impressed with his riding ability. Pete – who had won three saddles in the previous year, and knew that Mott's win didn't include one – gave up his trophy-saddle from the North American event, in a gesture of true magnanimity. He could have given Mott one of his old saddles, but that just wasn't Pete's way.

In Calgary, the impact of Pete Knight winning a bucking championship in distant Winnipeg was not lost on local reporters. The Calgary *Daily Herald* of July 7, 1926, trumpeted the details of the young Alberta cowboy's feat to its readership, beneath a headline that read, "Pete Knight Wins Another Trophy!"

To furnish the stock and the talent for this epic stampede, Peter Welsh's administrative talents were nearly taxed to their limits in the months leading up to the Dominion Day (later renamed Canada Day) affair in Manitoba. Welsh hired special train cars from the CPR to accommodate his purchase of carloads of horses captured from the last free-ranging four hundred-horse herd running wild in British Columbia's central caribou region. Twenty of the best riders from the Williams Lake range, including Shuswap Band Chief Joe Leonard, and renowned Caribou cowboy, Herb Matier, accompanied the newly-acquired Alberta Stampede Company bucking stock on the train to Winnipeg, via Lake Louise, Calgary, and Regina. From the Yakami Valley in Washington state, Welsh recruited another twenty-three American cowboys, who travelled eastward by automobile caravan via Coeur d'Alene, Idaho; Butte City and Billings, Montana; and Bismark, North Dakota, the group formally advertising the up-and-coming stampede as they travelled across the northern United States. The advance notice in those centres brought an influx of hundreds of American spectators to the stampede in Winnipeg. In Calgary, meanwhile, the competitors who had entered the saddle bronc bucking event were finishing a second day of elimination rides at the stampede.

The 'North American Open Saddle Bronc Riding' event coincided with the 'Canadian Saddle Bronc Riding' event at the Calgary Stampede, and both events were open to Canadian cowboys. An unknown nineteen-year-old bronc rider named Harry Knight travelled to Calgary to pay his entry fee and compete against a well-known cadre of top-notch, acclaimed bronc riders. Harry, who made his home in the cowboy-dominated tourist town of Banff, Alberta, was not related to Pete, and arrived at the stampede without a record of winning rides. Nevertheless, the young man drew tough, hard-bucking horses in the form of *Patch Face* and *Miles City* during the week's early elimination rides, and other men of known formidable reputation quickly extended a healthy respect toward the new arrival. Old hands of southern Alberta's stampedes, however, were not prepared for what would follow. Harry Knight's most spectacular ride of all was made on a horse named *One Buck*, before the critical eyes of stampede judges Jimmy Mitchell, Walter Deegan, and Emery La Grandeur.

Harry, who had appeared to be little more than a fresh-faced gap-toothed youngster, came out of the chute on the deadly *One Buck*, spurring his mount in a long, smooth rhythm from shoulder to flank, as the horse rocketed across the infield ground. While other, better-known cowboys were separated from their saddles, Harry stayed the course on the notorious bucking bronc he had drawn. Harry became an overnight sensation, winning the Prince of Wales Cup on his debut entry to the national championship competition, and taking first prize in the stampede's bareback-bucking event as well.

A rumor quickly began to circulate that Harry was Pete Knight's younger brother, and the belief that the two were related would persist in years to come. When Pete and Harry finally met – at the end of Calgary's Stampede Week of 1926 – the two bronc riders quickly became friends. As the months and years progressed after their first meeting, the two Alberta cowboys became life-long friends and formidable competitors against each other, often travelling to rodeos together across the length and breadth of North America, with one Knight winning the purse and the other Knight's point accumulation hovering close behind the winner's.

The concluding festivities for the 1926 Calgary Stampede were held at Calgary's opulent railroad hotel, 'The Palliser.' The party was paid for by the City of Calgary and hosted by Calgary's Mayor, George Webster. Pete Knight and many of his fellow riders from the Alberta Stampede Company arrived by train from Winnipeg that day, and were on hand for the Palliser Hotel's cowboy festivities that night. Pete's older sister Nellie was one of the Palliser's featured pianists, who joined in the celebration with him, as the Stetson-clad revelers danced the night away to an orchestra that finished playing at sun-up, the following morning.

In the weeks following the shows in Winnipeg and the Calgary Stampede, the Alberta Stampede Company's entire assemblage of horses and bronc riders was again entrained, bound for the city of Vancouver, on Canada's west coast. Another stampede competition was featured in Vancouver on August 12. The highly-publicized show drew many thousands of spectators, to watch a contest where Pete Knight and three other cowboys shared the second and third cash prizes, while the event's winner, Frank Wood of Ellensburg, Washington, took the grand prize.

Four days after the Vancouver show ended, and after as many days and nights of tedious journey on an east-bound train, the company's riders participated in the opening ceremonies of the Ottawa Stampede, held during Ottawa's Centenary Week beginning August 16th, 1926. Pete Knight was one of the featured riders in the Ottawa show, who performed for many members of parliament who were on hand for the city's one-hundredth anniversary celebration. Pete's newest friend and rising competition, Harry Knight, arrived in Ottawa to join the company's rid-

The Alberta Stampede Company
Dominion Day 1926
Pete Knight won the North American Bucking Championship, while British Columbia's Oliver Mott won the Canadian Bucking Championship.
Photo source: Harold Knight

ers as the show was beginning, after having performed at a stampede held in Banff National Park's Ptarmigan Valley, for the 'Trail Riders of the Canadian Rockies.'

On the final day of the Ottawa show, Pete Knight once again drew the notorious *Gravedigger*, and was unceremoniously bucked off for the first time in three years. As quick as a cat, Pete landed on his feet and was running, as the horse's hooves flailed by him. The pick-up rider drove *Gravedigger* from the infield, as Pete reached the safety of the infield chutes, waving his hat in response to the polite applause of the crowd. One of Pete's biggest competitors and long-time friend, Slim Watrin, won the Ottawa Stampede bucking event later that afternoon.

On September 25, the City of Toronto hosted its first 'International Western Stampede,' –an extravaganza organized by Welsh's stampede company – that drew thousands from across Ontario and the United States. The redoubtable *Midnight*, whose name headed a list of three hundred 'outlaw horses,' drew top billing in advertisements that also proclaimed a cast of one hundred 'real western cowboys.' Pete Knight and the company's other bronc riders gave exhibition performances

World's Championship
Winnipeg, Manitoba
Pete Knight can be seen wearing a white shirt and waving his Stetson as he stands astride a horse. Next to him in the dark shirt is friend and worthy competitor, Frank Sharp of High River Alberta.

Cowboy Contestants at Toronto Stampede
The Toronto Stampede, Sept 25-Oct 2, 1926
Those riding in the event are named. The 'civilians' at the centre of the photo are unnamed.
From left to right (left page):
Coyote Frank, Jim Mooney (standing), Sam Talkington, Buster Connelly, Slim Watrin, Leo Watrin, Casey Patterson (the Cowboy Mayor of Gadsby, Alberta), George McIntosh, Slim Leist, Bud Shaw, Earl Thode, Dick Raeburn, Jack Evans, Fred Hewitt, unknown, Fred Kennedy (the three to his left are unknown), Basil Allard, and George Hamilton. Behind the unnamed individuals are Frank Bennet, and Frank Sharp. Dick Cosgrave is standing on the chuckwagon.

each afternoon and evening in Toronto, before judges Sam Talkington, 'Slick' Reynolds, and Bob Carey.

It was the first time that anyone had ever brought a taste of the west to Toronto, and the city's citizens were in total awe of the cowboys. The Mayor of Toronto, Thomas Foster, led a Monday morning horse-mounted parade to Toronto's City Hall, with Bob Carey, Frank Sharp, Fred Kennedy, Earl Thode, and Pete Knight serving as his outriders. Behind Toronto's mayor, dozens of mounted members of the stampede company – all decked out in boots and chaps and Stetsons – rode down the city's avenues, while Torontonians waved and cheered to the western procession. At City Hall, the cowboys somberly stood before the Cenotaph while stampede Judge Bob Carey – who had been sent to France during the war with Alberta's Eighty-Ninth Battalion (Overseas) and had lost a leg at the Battle of the Somme – dedicated a wreath to the Canadian cowboys who had lost their lives in the conflict. Mayor Foster and his cowboy escort remounted and rode on through the streets of Toronto as thousands clapped and cheered, the horses' hooves beat-

Placing Wreath on Cenotaph at City Hall
The Alberta Stampede Co. Ltd.

Continuing left to right (right page):
Tom Foster (Mayor of Toronto), Jack Ault, Bob Carey, Peter Welsh (Owner of The Alberta Stampede Company), Miss Stastia Cross, Jack Cooper, Slim Polley, Pete Knight, Joe Fisher, Pete Vandermeer (the Prince of Wales Cowboy), Barney Hogg, Herb Matier and James Carey.
Photo source: Sharon and Herm Thielen – Jim Mooney Family Collection

ing loudly on the city's pavement as the procession returned to the exhibition grounds at a fast canter.

Pete Knight shared the first day-money for that Monday's bucking horse contest with Bob Askins of Montana, and Pete remained tied with Askins until the final day of the show. It was evident that Torontonians regarded the stampede with more than mild curiosity. On the last day of the Toronto performance, thirty thousands spectators attended the show at the Canadian National Exhibition grandstand, concluding performances that had seen one hundred twenty-five thousand spectators arrive throughout the week.

The finals in both of the bucking horse competitions – North American and Canadian – were held on a rain-soaked infield on Saturday, October 2. To break the tie held by the two leading riders, Pete Knight and Bob Askins were required to draw for a 'ride-off' in the North American bucking horse event. Askins drew *Midnight* and Pete drew *Bassano*, a horse of near-equal reputation to the big black gelding. Bob Askins blazed out of the chute on *Midnight* and remained with his mount in a spectacular ride that put him squarely in first place. Pete gave the crowd a hair-raising ride on *Bassano* and finished just three points behind Askins.

Although Pete's performance was relegated to a second-place finish in the North American event, he won the show's Canadian bucking event by a comfortable lead ahead of Frank Sharp and Slim Watrin.

The Toronto Stampede was declared a huge success by its organizers, with the awards being presented before a cheering crowd to Bob Askins, to Pete Knight and to a host of other cowboys by a strikingly-attractive Miss Toronto. On the Sunday following the end of the Toronto show, Peter Welsh's cowboys entrained again, this time heading for Montreal where a western stampede and rodeo would be presented for the first time to the people of Quebec.

The Montreal performance began on October 9, and was received with great enthusiasm by the local citizenry, who flocked to the make-shift stampede grounds at Delormier Park, to bear witness to 'the cowboys.' Montreal had never before witnessed such a spectacle. From the sold-out bleachers and despite the chill of mid-October setting in, grandstand patrons bundled up in long wool coats and snuggled beneath heavy wool blankets to cheer the procession.

By mere coincidence, Will Rogers, the half-Cherokee cowboy entertainer from Claremore, Oklahoma, was starring in his own show at 'His Majesty's Theatre' that weekend in Montreal. Rogers, a trick-roper and a former working cowboy from America's cattle states had become famous across North America for his dry wit and western charm. The star had a great affection for rodeo and was an enthusiastic fan at Welsh's stampede performances.

The prizes offered to the Alberta Stampede Company's competitors in the Chuckwagon, Roman Standing, and wild horse races – and for the premier event, the bucking horse competition with saddle – added up to a total of $20 000 in gold. When the price of gasoline was three cents for an imperial gallon, and a new men's suit sold for three dollars, the prize money offered to the cowboys was astonishing.

The show never lagged for thrills, excitement, or astounding feats of horsemanship. When Pete and his fellow riders had finished their competition performance, and were preparing the horses for the evening's performance, the brothers 'Tiny' and Alfie Welsh – aged nine and eleven – thrilled the crowd with their horse-jumping prowess, taking their mounts over six-foot obstacles without clipping a top-railing with a hoof.

Midnight – who had received the greatest billing in the newspapers after buck-ing off Bob Askins and Norman Edge – finally had his name drawn from the hat, by Pete Knight. Pete was finally given the opportunity to ride the coal-black 'streak of misery,' and the whispers began to circulate that evening, as the cowboys spoke about the draw and looked forward to witnessing the next day's battle between leg-endary horse and champion rider. They would finally get to see the ride they had all been speculating upon, and discussion worked late into the night, as the cow-boys smoked and chewed their tobacco and spoke of *Midnight* in hushed tones.

On the following afternoon, the big black gelding was brought from his stall – out through the corrals and into the chutes – having been haltered and quietly led by one of the young Welsh boys. *Midnight* was as docile as a house-pet, as long as no-one tried to saddle him up and ride him. Pete and two of the other cowboys gin-gerly placed Pete's saddle on the horse, and began cinching him down for the ride. The horse's ears came up and he tossed his head as he stood waiting.

When the chute gate squealed open on its heavy steel hinges, *Midnight* wast-ed no time; the powerful horse clearing the chute with his rider, bucking with a ferocity that Pete had rarely experienced before. As the horse's fore-hooves struck the ground a second time, the impact was such that Pete's ears were ringing and his nose began to bleed. By the horse's third lunge, however; Pete spurred the horse longer and harder – from shoulder to flank, again and again – in the pedaling, cyclic rhythm that had become his signature. With an iron-grip, he had the horse just where he wanted him – for all of three seconds. In the seventh second, *Midnight* suddenly whipped back to his right, as he bucked straight up and down in a semi-circle. Pete had lost his left stirrup and his balance for just a millisecond, long enough to cause him to be unseated on the next leap. Despite having taken the horse through the wildest eight seconds of his life, Pete could no longer keep his place in the saddle, and landed on his feet in the dusty infield as *Midnight* bucked away. Pete had disqualified in the ninth second.

When the ride prematurely ended, *Midnight* was bleeding from spur-cuts down both flanks, while the rider was hemorrhaging from his nostrils and lips, his mouth having been cut by his own teeth. Pete made his way back to the chutes, wiping blood from the huge grin on his face, as the crowd gave him a big round of applause for his effort. The horse had given him a ride for his money, and he knew then what he was up against if they met in the future.

In the years after the Montreal Stampede, Pete often claimed with no reserva-tion that *Midnight* was one of the toughest horses of his career to ride in competition. His old injury may have come back to haunt him at a critical moment, but he'd do everything in his power to prevent it the next time he met his nemesis.

Although Pete did not win the championship in Montreal, he had collected many of the day-winnings, throughout the week. He had finally been given his first opportunity to ride *Midnight* and give his appraisal of the legendary bucker. Fully recovered that night, Pete rode in the stampede on the last day, when the cowboys gathered to receive their winnings before a packed grandstand of cheering Montreal fans. After the stampede was postponed for a day due to cold, heavy rains, the show ended on Monday, October 18. The cowboys pitched in to lead bucking horses to transports; to load, feed, and haul tack and harness and chuck-wagons onto the trains. They said goodbye to the last city the stampede would perform in that fall.

Arena Director Fred Kennedy, conducted the company – Frank Sharp and Pete and Harry Knight, the Watrin brothers, the Welsh brothers, and dozens of other cowboys in the show's troupe – to a waiting CPR rail-car that would take them home to the west. Within an hour of the stampede ending and the prizes being awarded, heavy, wet flakes of snow began to fall on Montreal.

As their train passed over the great Canadian shield and meandered its way west onto the expanse of the prairies, bronc rider Jack Cooper, who had broken his right leg beneath a horse rolling in the mud, sat on pillows and train-seat cushions with a dozen other cowboys who had been previously hospitalized, and with dozens more who had not. Slim Watrin told a joke to a half-dozen listeners, with the punch-line causing all in ear-shot to roar with laughter, one cowboy wincing in pain as he laughed, from the tape restricting his broken ribs. Pete Knight was in his element, listening and laughing with the rest of the boys, as he spoke of *Midnight* and *Gravedigger* and the next year's stampede season, and roared his approval as another joke rolled off of another cowboy's tongue.

The Alberta Stampede Company's riders made the most of their trip home, playing cards, smoking hand-rolled cigarettes, and swapping yarns of bucking horses and winning rides; a season that had taken them from the Pacific coast to the St. Lawrence Seaway in five short months. Although none of their families had come with the cowboys on the epic trek across Canada, the Calgary *Daily Herald* newspaper was supplied with a steady stream of feats of derring-do performed by the cowboys, through the wire dispatches sent by Fred Kennedy. Pete's family – as with all the families of the other riders – was thus kept informed of the stampede company's successes across the country.

One young company bronc rider who rode west on a homeward-bound CPR train that October was Jim Mooney of Shepard, Alberta. Decades later, Jim would tuck his daughter Sharon into bed with late evening tales of the Stampede Company, and tell of riding before the Prime Minister of Canada in the greatest of stampedes that had ever been held in Ottawa, Toronto and Montreal. He spoke of the bucking horses, of the cheering crowds and of his close friendship with the legendary Pete Knight, his all-time greatest hero.

An era came to an end that week for cowboys everywhere, with the passing of the great western artist and famous cowboy of the old west, Charles M. Russell. A hero of Pete's and of cowboys everywhere – for the gift of his beautifully-rendered paintings of bucking broncs and the western plains – 'Charlie' Russell died in Great Falls, Montana, that snow-bound October of 1926. Charlie's passing made front-page news across the continent, and saddened every cowboy in the entire Alberta Stampede Company, as they read the local newspapers handed to them by the railroad's young black porters. As the cowboys' discussion revolved around Russell's famous paintings – "Bronc to Breakfast" being a comical favorite of Pete's – and the legend he had become, it was not realized at the time that their friend and comrade of the rodeo infield, Pete Knight, would soon become a legend in his own right.

6

Becoming a Legend

The 1927 Calgary Stampede began on July 11, kicking off with a Monday morning parade that was declared capable of out-doing all of those parades of previous years. The stampede events began that Monday in fast and efficient style, but the competitive riding for the afternoon was outdone by the contestants performing in their elimination rides on the following Tuesday. The cowboys had cast off their wooly angora chaps in favor of lighter cowhide, and the style of the Stetsons featured a narrower brim, but the horses were every bit as ferocious as they had been.

Pete Knight drew a horse named *C X Black*, and as horse and rider came thundering out of the chute, the bucking bronc came down hard on his hooves and proceeded to gyrate his way across the field toward a section of churned, dusty infield, directly in front of the grand-

Pete Knight with Award Saddle
Calgary Stampede, July 1927
The hand-tooled Johnny Foss saddle, from Riley and McCormick was just one of the many awards presented to Pete Knight after winning both the North American and the Canadian Bucking Championships.
Photo source: Glenbow Archives

stand. The contortions of *C X Black* provided a close-quarters display of Pete's expert riding ability for the paying crowd, and prompted the judges to score high points for his outstanding performance, in an opening round of the competition. Against notable riders such as Alf Hodgkins, George Copithorne, Sykes Robinson, and Miles Mabey – all having made their names and reputations at rodeos across southern Alberta – Pete's name was included in the semi-final list of rides to be performed later that week.

The North American Bucking event and the Canadian Championship Bucking event continued on their death-defying parallel course, as the contests between horse and man were played out before the grandstand crowd. Breezy Cox and Mike Stuart, both of Arizona, took the Wednesday first and second day-money for the North American, followed by two of the Watrin Brothers. A recent arrival to the Calgary Stampede's competition named Lee Ferris – better known to his friends as the 'Canada Kid' – took the top day-money for the Canadian Championship.

After a heavy rain fell on the Wednesday afternoon, Thursday's competition was performed in a sea of mud, as the riding events continued. Pete drew a horse named *Bow River Girl*, and was warmly cheered to round after round of enthusiastic applause, after performing another winning ride on a mount doing all in its power to be rid of its mud-bathed rider. In spite of Pete's outstanding performance, Americans 'Paddy' Ryan and Bobbie Askins took first and second day-money in the North American event, while Casey Patterson – the 'Cowboy Mayor' of small-town Gadsby, Alberta and a good friend of Pete Knight's – won the day-money for the Canadian Championship event.

The horses that carried the riders in their winning performances carried names that were often familiar to the spectator crowd, and some others were new additions to the stampede, either to be forgotten at the summer's end or remembered, paid tribute to, and eulogized for decades to follow. *Lonely Valley Grey, Hell to Sit, Good Enough, Una, High Roller,* and *Powder River* were among the names of these 'seasonal' horses that stock contractors introduced and cowboys drew to ride, in an event that the newspapers described as "navigation on the hurricane decks of wild horses."

The week that saw a veritable parade of contestants riding bucking horses to a successful finish was not without mishap, however. Casey Patterson was unceremoniously thrown into the infield mud and badly bruised. Moments later, Saint John's Ambulance attendants carried another cowboy, badly-injured and unconscious, from the infield.

For the final ride in the Canadian event, Pete Knight drew a horse named *Nightmare*, and the bronc did all he could to live up to his name. Bucking his way out of the rain-streaked chute and into a still-muddy infield, *Nightmare* put up the greatest fight of the afternoon in the event, with Pete's spurs flashing from shoulder to flank as the ten-second gun was fired and the cheering from the crowd reached a crescendo. Within the hour, Pete drew another horse named *Black Nitro*, for his competition ride in the North American event. A stationary bucker, *Black Nitro* took his rider straight up and down only a foot from the chutes, as cowboys hovering on the top rail leaned back and gave Pete a wide berth, to spur the coal-black bronc to a winning finalé. As the tenth second passed – again marked by gun-fire from beside the judge's platform – Pete was joined by the pick-up man, galloping up to his left side. Pete nimbly lofted himself off of *Black Nitro's* back, behind the pick-up rider's saddle-cantle, and down to the ground at a dead run on the far side of the pick-up horse, as the cheering from the crowd abated. Pete had been firmly in control on both rides, and his left ankle – the 'Achilles heel' that he constantly rode with – had not failed him in those critical moments. Other riders in both of the bucking events had appeared to surpass his performance that week, but Pete's hour of legendary acclaim had finally arrived.

As the points were tallied for the contestants' rides and the horses they had drawn, it was soon established beyond any doubt that Pete Knight had 'won all' in both premier bucking events, against the entire cowboy competition from across

Pete Knight presented with Prince of Wales Cup
Saturday, July 16, 1927.
Charles Murphy, General Manager of the Western Lines branch of the CPR presents the trophy
to Pete. It would be another six years before the cup would become Knight's outright.
Photo source: Glenbow Museum Archives

North America. For the first time, Pete's name would appear on a solid-silver plate beneath the 'Prince of Wales Cup.'

The Calgary *Daily Herald* edition for Monday, July 18, 1927, trumpeted the following declaration in bold type:

> Riding three of the worst outlaws that ever stepped in a stampede arena, Pete Knight of Crossfield, won both the Open and Canadian Bucking Horse Championships . . . before the greatest crowd in the history of the Calgary Exhibition and Stampede.

Pete Knight wins the Prince of Wales Cup for the first time
Calgary Stampede, July 1927
Guy Weadick, Pete Knight, and Charles Murphy
Photo source: Glenbow Museum Archives

The feat had never before been achieved in the young life of the Calgary Stampede, then in its seventh official year —and fifth consecutive year — of operation since the stampede's inception in 1912.

In the North American Open bucking event, Pete's lead was followed by Breezy Cox, Sykes Robinson and Slim Watrin, while in the Canadian Bucking event Slim Watrin, Sykes Robinson, and Harry Knight were named as the second, third and fourth-place winners respectively. Pete Bruised-head – the great Indian rider from Standoff, Alberta, who was admired by Pete Knight for his bucking ability – won the Canadian title that year for the calf-roping event.

Guy Weadick would declare that the boys in the events were "splendid," despite the difficulties of competing in the steady downpour and riding in sopping wet conditions, and that the judging had been the fairest that he had witnessed in any stampede to date.

After negotiating a rocky road of amateur competition, fracturing an ankle, sustaining dozens of bruises, bumps, scrapes, setbacks and five years of professional competition in the major stampedes of the day; for the first time, Pete Knight was finally declared the top rider not only in Canada, but across the length and breadth of North America, from Williams Lake, British Columbia to El Paso, Texas – and all in a single afternoon. The face of rodeo was changed forever on that day, and the bar of competition standards were raised considerably higher. Young people from across the west who had watched Pete Knight ride expressed their desire to be 'just like him,' often going home to farms and ranches and putting greater effort into their riding practices.

For future generations of cowboy contestants, many would enter a stampede arena, expressing a desire to ride like Pete. They climbed aboard wild, bucking horses, answering the challenge to all comers for the right to compete for the title of *North American Champion* or *Canadian Champion* bucking horse rider – in a contest that could very well take their lives in less than ten seconds.

Pet had won the championships, and as time went on, so too did the celebrations with cowboys from as far away as Texas congratulating their hero. Pete was invited from one gathering to the next in Calgary's Palliser, Yale, St. Regis, and Royal Hotels. Going home to the farm at Crossfield meant answering to a half-dozen supper invitations each week at neighboring farms. The Prince of Wales Cup and his other trophies sat in a corner in his brother Walt's living room, as Pete followed a beaten path on the rodeo trail for the rest of that summer.

In the days following the Calgary Stampede of 1927, the small town of Strathmore, Alberta, hosted a stampede that drew a crowd of thousands of spectators and many of the top contestants of the era, and featured a bucking competition that awarded one hundred dollars as its top prize. While the Strathmore show was taking place, the Hand Hills Lake Stampede began on the same afternoon, at a remote arena located fifteen miles east of Drumheller, Alberta. On the speculation that Hand Hills would have tougher bucking stock and a larger prize purse, Pete Knight entered that bucking event, competing against several cowboys of renowned ability.

Before a crowd of two thousand spectators, Pete came out of the chute on a bronc that appeared to be a wild bucker. The region had received a downpour the day before, and the infield had not yet dried. By the fifth jump, the horse fell in the slick muck of the arena, toppling onto his rider with his full weight. Pete was badly bruised in the aftermath of the wreck and limped from the field, as the next contestant's name was called. Pete was offered a re-ride, which he declined. Instead, Pete sat out the contest for the rest of the afternoon, attempting to work out the massive, painful bruising he had sustained. Horse liniment, stretching of extremities, and rags dipped in cool water – to be applied to torn muscles – were the only remedies at hand. No doctor was available that afternoon, nor often on any other day. Bronc riders were frequently left to their own devices for the healing of strains, sprains and bruises. Sleep in these circumstances was elusive, and waking the next morning was a renewed torture of torn muscles.

On the second day of the rodeo, in spite of the painful condition Pete was in, he drew a horse that carried him to first place in the Hand Hills Bronc riding event. On the same day, Pete's friend and fellow competitor from the 1924 Calgary Stampede finals, Cecil Henley, won the one hundred dollar prize at Strathmore.

In the week following the Strathmore and Hand Hills Lake rodeos, Pete again took to the dirt roads with his brother Walt, driving north more than a hundred miles to enter the bucking horse event at the Gadsby Stampede, located east of the larger centre of Stettler, Alberta. In spite of suffering from extensive bruises to his upper body and the strain he had sustained in his left shoulder and bucking hand, Pete drew the horse named *Tornado* – reputed to be the toughest horse of the show – and won first place in the three-day event while riding against Casey Patterson and Slim Watrin, who won second and third places in the contest. And always, the small-town stampede received huge support and patronization from thousands of paying spectators, arriving after many miles of travel on the open prairie to cheer for their favorite bronc riders.

While values of the inhabitants of the eastern provinces and states held to sedate business and living practices, development of schools and universities, and to notions of managing the entire continent from eastern boardrooms, westerners were still very much akin to their frontier roots. The businesses that evolved from those origins reflected squarely upon those roots. Honor and honesty to the people and to the land was a foremost notion for westerners, held higher than the pursuit of parliament and finance prevalent in the east. The consciousness of westerners was steeped in self-reliance; business practices founded on the bedrock of a man's word and his handshake, and a genuine love for the wide, open spaces found in North America's western states and provinces. Cowboys who rode the region's most notorious horses were, and would always be, a westerner's idolized hero.

Rural stampedes were to be found virtually everywhere in southern and central Alberta during the 1920's. Horses and other livestock were abundant, spectators were keen supporters, and admission to any stampede was cheap enough to be reasonably affordable entertainment for a family. The contestants were competing in events that reflected skills they had honed while working on farms and ranches across the western United States and Canada, skills appreciated and respected by their spectators and fans. The bonding of the cowboy culture and the spectatorship and support that followed this culture created a consciousness that had almost nothing in common with the east, or with eastern governments and their values. It was as if a new country within the borders of the existing two countries had aligned itself from Alberta to Texas, and the people who lived in this corridor created a culture that corresponded with the notional absence of national boundaries, and made every attempt to practice that friendship.

Pete Knight had won top honors at the most prestigious stampede in Canada, and had thrilled millions of his fellow citizens and rodeo fans from around the globe, in just a few short years. From the American cowboys he had met in his travels across Canada, and from the stories they brought to Alberta of riding bucking horses down south, Pete was beginning to realize that bigger rodeos and greener pastures existed over the horizon – in his birthplace, the United States of America.

7
Busting Down Borders

The City of Columbus, Ohio hosted its second annual rodeo and stampede to coincide with the Ohio State Fair, during the first week of September, 1927. The Alberta Stampede Company hired special trains to ship its troupe of one hundred cowboys, three hundred horses and all of the equipment needed to perform the Ohio show. The cash prizes being offered were, once again, enormous by any standard, and the young, eager, and highly-talented contestants looked forward to sharing in the twenty thousand dollars put up by the company.

The population of Columbus received the stampede with a mixture of curiosity and enthusiasm. An average of fifty thousand spectators filed through the fairground turnstiles each day, astounding numbers by Canadian standards. Bronc riding representatives from two continents, including Australia's Allen McPhee, Arizona's own Breezy Cox, and Canada's Walter Armsdon, thrilled the grandstand crowd to a world-class performance of bronco busting.

This was Pete Knight's first competition 'south of the line,' and he found it thrilling to be back in the land of his birth and riding for an appreciative American audience. As a special treat for the crowd and for a bonus of five hundred dollars in added prize money, the contestants first rode in the Australian-style on flat English saddles, and then in an American-style competition, using the standard American cowboy saddle. The horses received top billing, with *Gravedigger, Yellow Fever, Midnight* and *Five Minutes to Midnight* being the foremost in a list of 'bad' horses that numbered in the dozens. The local newspaper, *The Columbus Dispatch,* declared, "It takes real men to ride 'em!" as the last bronc bucked his rider onto the Columbus infield sawdust, and the show came to a finalé under a rolling blanket of thundering applause.

Pete Knight was declared the winner in the Columbus Stampede bucking contest. Pete had drawn the redoubtable *Gravedigger,* and was learning to sense where this horse would go in his wildly-kicking gyrations. Nevertheless, Pete had a handful beneath him, as *Gravedigger* did all he could to try to dump his rider. It was a rough ride but this time, Pete triumphed and was followed in 'points accumulated' by his long-time friend, Frank Sharp, who drew *Midnight* and bucked the horse into a wild second-place finish.

After the Columbus show had ended, the Alberta Stampede Company quickly boarded a train and headed north to Montreal, in the province of Quebec. In the weeks leading up to October 1, 1927, Montreal's newspaper reporters wrote, "The best aggregation of bucking horses ever drawn together in any part of the world" were being featured at a stampede in the Montreal Forum. It was one of the first times in Canada that a stampede would be held indoors.

Peter Welsh, who orchestrated the advent of a Montreal Stampede, featured his show-billing locally under the heading of the "Stamrod Company," and delivered to Montreal a small army of cowboys and builders, who were given the job of preparing the Montreal Forum for the contest to be held there. Chutes were built, tons of earth were hauled into the makeshift infield, and sawdust was laid as a finishing touch upon which the stampede's events would be performed. Surrounding the infield, a six-foot steel fence was erected to protect the paying crowd. With the preparations completed, opening day saw a packed Forum as Francophones and Anglophones were treated to the thrills of a western stampede.

The show was rolling along at a fast pace, as each event played out before an appreciative packed forum. Each horse coming from a chute blazed across the infield in a flurry of dust, while his rider made every attempt to hang on.

While all was going according to plan, a bucking bronc suddenly plunged over the steel fence that separated the spectators from the infield, with his rider left hanging onto the top railing. Still kicking and pawing his way over the rail, the horse nearly landed in the laps of the closest spectators. Panic erupted and people scrambled over their seat-backs – and over neighboring spectators – in an effort to avoid the seemingly-crazed horse. Kenneth T. Dawes, the Canadian President of the Society for the Prevention of Cruelty to Animals (SPCA), and his friend Arthur Ross, manager of the Boston Bruins hockey club, both sat in the front row and joined the scramble to get away from the horse. The bolting bronc was quickly subdued by the pick up rider and driven away to the stock corrals. The panic dissipated and the spectators claimed they were shaken but unhurt. Everyone in the forum had received a thrill beyond expectation, and the pandemonium drew a ripple of nervous laughter after all the spectators involved had regained their seats. The SPCA president later endorsed the Montreal Stampede's performances, advising reporters that the treatment he had witnessed of the animals in the rodeo events fell completely within the guidelines of his organization.

Rodeos on the western prairies had ended long before September, so the autumn of 1927 heralded another late rodeo season for Pete and the other company riders. Pete was experiencing his first taste of the American reception to rodeo, after competing in Detroit, Buffalo, and Columbus. Witnessing some of the sights and sounds that America had to offer stirred vague memories, from his early years spent in the southern states. America had the biggest crowds he had ever seen, and cowboys he met spoke of longer-established rodeos in all of the western or 'cattle states.' Professional-level class-A rodeo contests – not only those held by the Alberta Stampede Company – were held in many eastern cities whose populations hungered for a brief nostalgic look at the western events that had helped to shape the American frontier. For Pete, the realization of his dream to live as a bucking-horse rider in the modern world was finally coming true. As time progressed, fewer ties held Pete to his father's farm or to his own farmland, and the winter of 1927-28 would leave him fully in charge of his affairs.

In a three-year succession leading up to the fall of 1928, Pete's land was beset with crop failure, due to early frost. His income from winning the bucking horse contest at even one stampede was often more than a farmer could make in eight months of farming and feeding cattle. The rodeo winnings were a welcome relief to Pete, enabling him to live well and still pay for his failing farm. Brothers Robert and Walt encouraged Pete to carry on with his rodeo successes, and they in turn would continue to farm his section of land in addition to their own properties. It was an agreeable arrangement that benefited all.

As the winter drew on, tragedy once again struck the Knight family. Pete's father, William – having lived on his own for nearly a year after Katherine Knight's passing – had assumed a habit of moving from Robert's farm to Walt's, where he would live with one son's family until his mood changed and a sudden compulsion would drive him to move in with the other son. On one such occasion, William walked alone from Robert's farm to Walt's, down roads choked with wet snow and calf-deep mud. Stubbornly marching on through a flooded creek ford – an unseen figure struggling across the vast emptiness of the landscape, in the solitude of a prairie afternoon – William was completely soaked when he arrived at Walt Knight's farm house. Deathly ill with pneumonia, William died two weeks later, as the spring of 1928 was ending.

With William's passing, Pete stayed as an alternating guest between Robert's and Walt's homes, when he wasn't tearing along a dirt highway at high speed in his newest Model T to arrive in time to yet another distant rodeo. He'd smashed up his last car the year before, after failing to negotiate a curve at high speed which resulted in blowing two tires simultaneously off of one side in the ensuing skid.

Pete's three-year tenure with Peter Welsh's Alberta Stampede Company ended after the corporation was dissolved and its assets sold off. The cowboys were all thanked for their participation, dedication, and skill in a venture that had brought fame to Alberta and considerable wealth to the top riders in the company. The bucking horses, *Midnight* and *Five Minutes to Midnight,* – along with dozens of other less-notable horses – were sold to American rodeo producer Colonel Jim Eskew. The two famous horses were in turn sold to Eddie McCarty & Vern Elliott, contractors to Cheyenne's Frontier Days Rodeo.

The press devoted many columns of type to the bucking contest in the days leading up to the 1928 Calgary Stampede. Local reporters declared in bold, black type that the event would be a 'Battle Royal' between Pete Knight of Crossfield and Bob Askins, the champion rider for the United States. There were, however, "many a slip between a cup and a lip," and those named cowboys did not finish in the top positions; not even Pete.

Rodeo historians and cowboys remember 1928 as the year the stampedes of southern Alberta were dominated by the three Watrin brothers, with a fourth brother in training and awaiting his day to compete in the big stampede.

In the Tuesday elimination rides at the Calgary Stampede, Pete won second-place day money behind Joe Fisher of Kew, Alberta, in the North American bucking event, as well as the day's first-place in the Canadian bucking event. The ride that Pete performed on the final day of that year's stampede would aid in solidifying the legend of Pete Knight's sheer brute ability at successfully kicking out a rank bucking bronc, under almost any circumstance. On Saturday, July 14, 1928, in a contest that was fought out by eight American and eleven Canadian finalists, a horse named *Too Bad* erupted from the chute with Pete spurring him on in a withering onslaught of spurs from shoulder to flank. The bronc was kicking and spinning in fine style, with Pete making a spectacular balanced ride, when *Too Bad* went 'over the top' and somersaulted forward onto his back before a mesmerized crowd of twenty thousand spectators – rolling directly over Pete in the process. The horse came up from the somersault, kicking and bucking after literally tumbling forward through the infield dust before thousands of shocked grandstand witnesses. Shock reverberated through the crowd when it quickly became clear to the judges and to all who were there that day, that Pete Knight had incredibly remained in the saddle, had not lost a stirrup and continued to spur the tumbling, rolling bronc with a grim determination, to finally master the bucking horse.

The feat of somersaulting a wild, bucking horse and remaining in the saddle had never before been seen by anyone in attendance, or even *heard* of by the cowboys who stood in awe and shook their heads in disbelief. The crowd went wild, leaving their seats as they cheered a frenzy of encouragement and appreciation to Pete, without realizing that their hero had badly torn all of the muscles across his chest and upper arms. Despite the phenomenal somersault, and having made good rides in the semi-finals and in the final competition on four outstanding horses, Pete narrowly missed achieving the top position in the Canadian bucking event; his points accumulated placing him a close second-place behind Leo Watrin.

While his brother carried away the Prince of Wales Cup for 1928, Slim Watrin won the North American bucking event,

Pete Knight on *Too Bad*

Miraculously, Pete managed to make a qualifying ride in spite of tearing his chest and upper arm muscles after staying on the horse through a somersault.

Photo source: Glenbow Archives

the Chrysler Trophy put up by Calgary's Imperial Motors, and the one thousand dollar prize that went with it. Slim also won third place in the Canadian bucking event, followed by the now eminently-confident Harry Knight of Banff. Behind Slim Watrin's lead in the North American bucking event, Breezy Cox, Joe Fisher, and Sykes Robinson took the remaining three positions. In spite of a torn shoulder and chest muscles hampering his ability to compete, Pete continued to draw and ride the broncs that kept him in the running, but had little luck impressing the judges.

One cowboy contestant, 'Buster' Connelly of Lundbreck, Alberta, had not been so lucky during the week of riding competition. An initially good ride quickly went sour; Connelly was thrown and struck in the head with a flying hoof, sustaining a skull fracture in the process. Lingering near death for several days, Connelly's condition slowly began to improve by week's end, but the cowboy's bronc riding career was seriously curtailed. Spectators viewed serious injuries to be inevitable for most rodeo cowboys, and the determinant that would eventually end their bronc riding careers. Pete knew how fortunate he had been, while taking on the toughest horses on the continent and surviving relatively unscathed.

The acclaimed 'toughest horses' to ride, in the saddle-bronc bucking event of that year's stampede were *Too Bad*, *I Be Dam* and *Pop Again*, all top-ranking bucking horses that were featured at other rodeos and stampedes of the late 1920's and early 30's.

Canada's Governor-General, The Viscount Willingdon and his wife, Lady Willingdon, were on hand to present the Prince of Wales Cup and the other awards to the winners of the 1928 Calgary Stampede.

In the week following the stampede at Calgary, Leo Watrin again beat out Pete Knight, winning the bucking horse event at the Strathmore Stampede, and in the week following that event, Slim Watrin won the bucking horse contest at the Benalto Stampede, near the small city of Red Deer, Alberta.

The town of Olds, Alberta, put on a stampede at Billy Coates's private arena, two miles north of the small farming centre. Billy invited his friend Pete Knight to compete in the bucking contest, and Pete in turn stayed at the Coates ranch for the duration of the two-day show, winning first prize in the bucking contest. With a few hours of friendly contact making memories for a lifetime, Billy remembered the legendary bronc rider with a great fondness, for the rest of his long life.

Everyone who met Pete admired his amiable, polite manner, but even so, he was not above bruising egos or offending sensitivities with a temper that was kept in check. There were times when Pete's passion over an injustice bubbled to the surface, and he couldn't remain silent. More than once, Pete became embroiled in an argument where tempers flared, and voices were raised. On these rare occasions, the thunder of his sudden outburst carried far more weight, as his reputation for being mild mannered and polite preceded him everywhere he went. Pete buying 'drug store eye-glasses' for the Calgary Stampede judges was one such incident.

There was almost always some amount of question and criticism about the way a particular ride or a certain horse was marked by the stampede's judges, and there were as many opinions as cowboys to voice them. On a well-remembered afternoon after a bucking event ended in Calgary, Pete became embroiled in an argument with one of the judges. With a sudden flare of temper over an apparently skewed judging decision, Pete had a clenched fist gripping the judge's shirt-collar and hauled him half-way out of the judging booth, high over the infield. The argument came to a sudden end, when nearby cowboys and judges pulled the two apart. Pete, however, would not let the matter end on the stampede's infield. That evening, he bought three sets of drugstore spectacles and presented them to the judges, in the company of a dozen other cowboys. The witnessed presentation – delivered as a solemn affair to three supposed 'blind men' – was not well-received by men the Calgary Stampede board considered expert in their collective ability and fair in their individual opinions. The 'gifts' were considered to be rude, unsporting, and delivered in poor taste. The movers and shakers in the stampede cautioned Pete indirectly that 'gifts' such as these could lead to his expulsion from the bucking event. The matter blew over and the stampede continued on its historical course, but the point had been made and the incident was never completely forgotten. Contestants often referred to a judge needing glasses, with a wink and smile, even decades later.

Among the dignitaries and tourists who arrived in Calgary for the 1929 stampede was an entourage headed by U.S. Grant, Jr., of San Diego, California. Grant, a son of the former United States President and famous Union Army General of the American Civil War, spoke in glowing terms of the city of Calgary, and made it known that the city owed its renown in his part of the world to the existence of the Calgary Stampede, and to the men and women who made the stampede a reality.

The stampede retained the judges of the former year – Carey, Mitchell, and La Grandeur – who would witness a hotly-contested bucking horse competition at that summer's stampede, and the arrival of a host of vaguely-familiar names from south of the border who would attempt to make their mark in Canada's premier stampede contest.

Pete Knight, who had won the High River bucking contest the week prior, was favored on the judge's list to win top honors at the 1929 Calgary Stampede. By Friday, the semi-final rides had been scored on such a narrow margin that the top North American bucking event day-money had to be split between American cowboys Earl Thode of South Dakota, and Gene Ross of Arizona. In the Canadian Bucking event on the same day, Harry Knight, Frank Sharp, Pete Knight, and twenty-two year old Herman Linder, of Cardston, Alberta, were all tied for first place, and these cowboys split the day-money four ways. Harry Knight also won fourth place day-money in the North American event. The contest was decided on the following day, with Earl Thode winning the North American Championship and young Herman Linder winning the Canadian Championship and the Prince of Wales Cup. In a close second place behind Linder was Pete, followed by Harry

Pete Knight from Crossfield, Alberta, riding at the Calgary Stampede
July, 1929

Photo source: Glenbow Archives

Knight, and Leo Watrin. Harry also won the runner-up position in the North American bucking event, while Pete won fourth place in that event, bringing his accrued winnings to four hundred fifty dollars for the two bucking events, in a competition that could not have been consistently closer throughout the week.

Two weeks after the Calgary Stampede ended, the biggest rodeo south of the Canada-U.S. border was held in Cheyenne, Wyoming. Cheyenne's thirty-third annual Frontier Days Rodeo, haled as being "The Daddy of 'Em All" and the greatest bucking horse event in the great state of Wyoming, began the last week of July, 1929. For the first time in many years, only two men made qualifying rides on the show's bucking broncs, while another four highly-rated cowboys were tossed into the infield dirt and disqualified. Fred Stillings of Oregon claimed the Cheyenne bucking horse championship, with Pete Knight representing Calgary in the runner-up position. Although Pete was disappointed that his point score was not higher in the competition, he welcomed the challenge of a contest against the best riders the United States had to offer, on the best bucking horses that Wyoming stock contractors, Elliot & McCarty, could provide. Pete's determination to ride and to master the toughest horses – even to the detriment of his point standing – was his abiding, unwavering star of reference.

For the remainder of the summer and long into the autumn of 1929, Pete's name was to be found on the money list of nearly every major stampede and rodeo on the North American continent. Pete won Oregon's Pendleton 'Round-up' as the first Canadian ever to do so. That year found Pete riding the broncs in the

Ellensburg Rodeo in Washington State, the Roswell Rodeo in New Mexico, the Moose Jaw Stampede in Saskatchewan, and the Madison Square Gardens Rodeo in New York City – these being only a few of the rodeos he rode in. For all of the places that Pete travelled, it was inevitable that eventually someone somewhere would finally turn Pete Knight's head. Her name was Ida Lee, better known as 'Babe.'

Babe (Ida Lee) Knight
Photo source: Harold Knight Collection

8
The Heart of a Cowboy

In 1930, Spring heralded the rodeo season into Texas, as it did each year and still does today. After competing in the elimination rides at the Fort Worth show, Pete was invited to the wedding celebration of one of the local cowboys. At the reception Pete met the cowboy's bride, Peggy Avant Seate, and was introduced to her petite twenty-one year old sister Ida – known to her friends and family as 'Babe.' Pete and Babe were cordial to one another, but their worlds appeared to be completely opposite to one another's.

Babe was the daughter of prominent Hot Springs businessman Thomas Avant, and Pete, in spite of his growing fame, was a professional rodeo cowboy who travelled back and forth across the continent as a matter of course. The life of any serious rodeo contestant was a nomadic existence, like a carney in a travelling circus. Nevertheless, there was a strong attraction between the cowboy from Crossfield and the society girl from the Ouachita Mountains, and when the wedding celebration for Babe's sister ended, the two parted on friendly terms. Both knew, if they ever did meet again, it may not be for a very long time to come. So with his focus trained on the profession Pete had set before himself, the young cowboy put aside thoughts of romance and once again travelled north to the biggest bucking horse contest in Canada – the Calgary Stampede.

Pete quickly nodded his head to the chute man, and as the gate swung open, *Calico* sprang forward and upward, as if fired from the muzzle of a cannon. With great, twisting leaps, the horse bucked and spun across the infield, while Pete maintained his balance in the saddle and spurred the horse to victory.

For the second time in his life, Pete Knight won the Prince of Wales Cup. The newspapers trumpeted to their readers that Pete was indeed Canada's Premier Bronc Rider, over the Watrin Brothers, the one-eyed Lee Ferris – a.k.a. Canada Kid – Frank Sharp, and a host of other renowned Canadian and American bronc riders. Pete's lead in the Canadian bucking event was narrowly followed by brothers Leo and Slim Watrin's exceptional rides. They took second and third place in the event, with the Canada Kid finishing in fourth place.

Pete Knight was the first bronc rider to place his name on the Prince of Wales Cup, *twice*. For those cowboys who had missed adding their names to the trophy even once, the cup seemed like a distant dream, and for those who had captured the cup once before, the odds of winning a second time were a long-shot. Since the stock crash of the previous year, the huge cash prize that went with the Canadian Championship had dwindled to a mere fraction, but the prestige of winning the cup – for cowboys experiencing leaner times, and expecting more ahead – became more focused. Every contestant was now speculating on Pete's chances of taking the cup as his own at next year's stampede.

'Chuck' Wilson of Fort Worth, Texas, captured the North American bucking Championship, with Pete Knight claiming the runner-up position. Pete drew a horse named *Powder Pin*, a bronc that refused to buck as hard as Wilson's horse. As a result, *Powder Pin* lost points for his rider, leaving Pete confident that he could have taken the North American event, had he drawn a tougher horse. Brothers Eddie and Leo Watrin placed third and fourth in the event, while riders such as Harry Knight and Slim Watrin were bucked off or lost stirrups, quickly becoming disqualified.

Counterfit – another horse Pete drew in the course of the week – gave his rider and the paying crowd a brilliant display of bucking ferocity. The photograph taken of Pete on *Counterfit* that afternoon became a perfectly-balanced image of horse and rider hovering in the air, and would in time assist in solidifying Pete's enduring fame. Two weeks after the Calgary Stampede ended, Pete Knight won the bucking horse contest at Cheyenne, taking the 1930 'Daddy of 'Em All' by storm.

Pete's reputation had begun to build on the American side of the 49th parallel that summer, with his victory at Cheyenne's Frontier Days Rodeo. Cheyenne was, and still is today, the greatest western pageant in North America, outclassing even the Calgary Stampede. It began its first season in the summer of 1897, after the bustling Wyoming town was urged by Union Pacific Railroad promoters to hold a 'western-style' celebration to draw the interest of rail tourists from the eastern United States. The exhibition and rodeo survived long after the big American rodeos of the 1930's had faded from memory. Far into the twenty-first century, stock contractors and rodeo personalities still commented on Cheyenne's success, and attributed its longevity to the simple reason that the Frontier Days Rodeo was a living, breathing entity unto itself. It thrived in the very heart of a wild-west environment and featured an annual entry of over fourteen hundred contestants from across North America.

After winning the Frontier Days Championship, Pete was paid fifty dollars to perform an exhibition ride as a finalé to the show's bucking event – on *Midnight*. As Pete came thundering out of the chute to the cheering of Cheyenne's spectatorship, he was able to hang on to the great, black 'bucking fury' for just seven and one-half seconds, until the legendary Alberta horse piled his rider into the infield dust. It was written long after that Pete was paid to take a 'dive' at Cheyenne's exhibition ride of 1930 – to add to the reputation of the legendary horse – and that the seven-ought second ride was staged. The great *Midnight* needed no such help, however, and Pete's reputation for honesty was far above the practice of that kind of deception, in spite of the persistent rumor that Pete had been paid one hundred dollars to 'fall off' of the horse during the exhibition ride. Pete told his brother Walt and nephew Harold shortly afterward that indeed, the money was offered beforehand for such a stunt, but that he had ridden the horse in an honest ride, without agreeing to take a dive or accepting a fee afterward. Integrity was a part of Pete's character.

Pete's exhibition ride on *Midnight* after winning the Fronter Days Bucking Championship.

Cheyenne, Wyoming
1930

*Photo source:
Harold Knight
Collection*

From Wyoming, Pete headed east and south, looking for other big rodeos to compete in, for whatever prize money was being offered at these small shows. The small city of Deadwood, South Dakota – a famous frontier town that had known personalities such as Wyatt Earp, 'Wild Bill' Hickock and 'Calamity' Jane – hosted a rodeo that summer, where Pete Knight spurred bucking horses past the plane of the Black Hills community's chutes. Later, Pete headed west and south, to compete in the bronc riding event at Monte Vista, Colorado. Monte Vista was the home town of World Heavyweight Boxing Champion, Jack Dempsey, and featured the state's oldest professional rodeo. From these contests, Pete drove hard to arrive at other rodeos in time to pay his entry fee; Visalia and Sonora, in California, on the Canada-United States border at Sumas, Washington, and still farther north and east to Moose Jaw, Saskatchewan.

On Thursday, August 28, 1930, Oregon's twenty-first annual Pendleton 'Round-up' began with a parade which included over one thousand cowboys and nearly two thousand native riders decked out in full traditional regalia, all proudly participating in the pomp, ceremony, and pageantry from eight separate nations across the American west. Twenty thousand people had arrived to witness yet another thrilling contest of the greatest cowboy competitors from across North America. The spectators included William Gibbs McAdoo, former secretary of the United States Treasury and California's candidate for the United States Senate. McAdoo's chartered aircraft from Portland brought the former statesman to the edge of the arena grounds, from which he strutted into a waiting crowd of well-wishers. He was dressed in a ten-gallon Stetson, wing-tip dress shoes, and golfing trousers!

Stock contractor Verne Elliott and his ubiquitous partner, Eddie McCarty, supplied the bucking horses to Pendleton that year. Elliott, who had been a featured contestant in the Cheyenne bucking Bison event of 1910, had introduced side-release chutes to Wyoming rodeos as early as 1927; McCarty was a well-known bronc rider of formidable reputation, who had won the bucking event at Cheyenne, in 1919. Pete had met Verne and Eddie only three years prior, but had formed a solid friendship with the two famous contractors. McCarty & Elliott also featured Pendleton's Northwest bucking contest – designated as a junior-grade competition for local riders – in addition to supplying Pendleton's World-class bucking championship horses, including *Midnight*. Bucking broncs that carried names such as *Big Munn*, *Strip*, *Saxet* and *Bally Sowers* may have all been assessed to be easy buckers for junior-level competition, but in each case these horses bested their riders in the local bucking contest.

When the points were tallied at the end of the third day of competition, Pete Knight, listed by reporters as representing Calgary, Alberta, was declared the winner of Pendleton's 'World' Bucking Championship, although the term was loosely applied and carried no official recognition outside of the United States.

In a death-defying contest of man versus horse, Pete captured a half-dozen runner-up victories, various North American and Canadian championships, won the Canadian Championship and Prince of Wales Cup twice, the North American title once at the Calgary Stampede, an all-American Championship at Cheyenne and now, a 'World' Class Championship in Oregon. Pete's fame was not just relegated to Canada alone, but his name was now synonymous with 'Champion Bronc Rider' across the entire Canadian and American west. He had yet to be officially declared, however, the 'World's Champion,' in his profession. Without a doubt, Pete had been tough on himself and even tougher on the horses he drew, and that toughness had finally paid off. He had arrived on a plateau attained by few men in his profession, but his fame and the challenges he faced each day were still growing. Across North America, Pete would continue to harvest bronc riding points at dozens of rodeos, that year.

It was in the spring of 1931 that Pete once again met Babe Avant, while Babe was visiting her sister Peggy at the height of rodeo week in Fort Worth. The sisters were part of a 'rodeo-wife' following, when everyone in their circle of friends socialized as a group. It had been a whole year since Pete had last seen petite, vivacious Babe Avant, and he thought her more beautiful than he'd remembered. There were no promises made or requested between the two, but it was clear Babe still had the ability to attract Pete Knight's attention. She was undeniably drawn to Pete's great sense of humor, his rugged good looks and the deep respect he commanded from everyone associated with rodeo. For Pete, Babe was the nicest girl he had ever met, and his mind was already made up. He was, however, just a little bit shy. When the Fort Worth Rodeo ended and the boys prepared to leave for the next big show, Babe and Pete were already wondering when they would see each other again. Pete, experienced as a professional cowboy, was not a romantic young man, but Babe would change that, in time.

Pete's awesome riding ability and personal brute strength was again presented that year, to a crowd of admiring spectators at the 1931 Calgary Stampede. He did not win the final prize in either of the bucking events that week, but his growing number of fans witnessed a ride that left them breathlessly cheering, in awe and admiration of the young bronc rider's talent. On the first Monday of the stampede, Pete drew *Alberta Kid*, the chunky Bay that had weathered seven previous stampedes while shrouded in the acclaim of being one of the toughest bucking horses of the decade. After exploding from the chute, the horse shook Pete 'off balance' on the fourth leap. Despite being loosened from his position on the horse's back, Pete literally kicked himself back into the saddle, while spurring the horse high in the mane and far back along the flanks. Again in full control of his buck-rein, his saddle, and his balance – with spurs flashing down each side of the horse in the afternoon sun – Pete rode *Alberta Kid* to a standstill before a madly-cheering crowd, to win the first prize day-money in the event. It was a ride that Pete had wished Babe could have seen, if only to fortify his assurance to her that he wouldn't be injured by a bucking horse.

The ride captured the collective attention of a prairie province struggling in the throes of a crushing depression, and was just one more example of faith people needed, that a 'come-back' could be the rule and not the exception. The stampede's judges were hard-pressed to recall a more memorable ten seconds. Newspaper reporters described the ride as spectacular, in the extreme, and even the judges joined in the rousing applause – an unprecedented act of paying homage to a truly formidable display of horsemanship.

On the following Wednesday, Pete drew a horse named *Pistol Pete* in the Canadian bucking event and lost his stirrup on the fifth jump, disqualifying him from the event. This left the remaining North American event open to Pete, but he never made it past the semi-finals. On the Friday afternoon Pete drew *Strathmore Girl* and was unceremoniously bucked off on the sixth leap the horse made. It was a bad week for former champions, as Harry Knight was sent to Calgary's General hospital with internal injuries, while Bobby Askins was disqualified for losing a stirrup in the semi-finals. Slim Watrin won the Prince of Wales Cup, the railroad trophy sponsored by Canadian Pacific Railway Chairman, E.W. Beatty, and seven hundred fifty dollars that accompanied the Canadian championship. The pinch of a nation-wide depression was particularly felt in rodeo competition, where the big money prizes of the 1920's were truly a thing of the past. The North American championship and the Hoot Gibson trophy went to Oklahoma's Gene Ross, after he had performed an exceptional ride on *Mountain Boy* before an admiring crowd of southern Albertans. From Calgary, Pete headed south to Cheyenne.

The greatest names in rodeo arrived in Cheyenne for the five-day battle between world-class champions, Pete Knight among them. The thirty-fifth annual 'Daddy of 'Em All' rodeo kicked off on Tuesday, July 21, 1931. Pete Knight and his old friend and competitor from the summer of 1924, Cecil Henley, talked rodeo while lining up to pay their entry fees at the registration window. Pete drew the contestant number eighty, while Cecil was assigned contestant number eighty-one. With names such as Earl Thode, Earvie Collins, and Gene Ross on the docket, the week promised to be a series of pitched battles between cowboy contestants. Turk Greenough won the day-money on the first afternoon of the contest. On day two, Pete drew a horse named *Co Ed* and took the day-money in a win the young Alberta cowboy worked hard to achieve. Thursday's program was won by the exceptionally talented Earl Thode on *School Girl*, while all nine hundred pounds of little *Five Minutes to Midnight* sent the Canada Kid (Lee Ferris) rocketing from the saddle into a cloud of infield dust.

By Friday, the program of semi-final contestant riders had been published, and the cowboys prepared to buck the horses they had drawn, one by one. Pete drew a horse of tough reputation named *Patches*, but performed nothing more than a fast gallop on him, thereby winning a re-ride. In the re-ride, however, *Golden Rule* literally bucked Pete into the second-place day-money, thus assuring his eligibility in the final contest the following day. Harry Knight made the most popular ride that afternoon on the wicked, little *Five Minutes to Midnight*.

As Saturday afternoon unfolded, Earl Thode came out of the chute on *Five Minutes to Midnight* and rode the horse to an outstanding finalé, securing the 1931 Cheyenne bucking championship. Pete Knight drew the wily *Invalid*, often referred to as a carbon-copy of the legendary *Midnight*. With the horse bucking with a bone-jarring intensity, Pete captured the runner-up position behind Thode.

When the afternoon's bucking event concluded and the winner was announced, the time came for the 'exhibition ride' performance by the champion bronc rider. Earl Thode came out of the chute on *Midnight* in a great leap of bucking horse-hide, spurring the bronc with a practiced fluidity as he gripped the buck-rein with one clenched fist. On the horse's third jump, Thode was sent flying into the air. The unwinged Pegasus had bested yet another champion rider. Cowboys could ride to championships, but *Midnight* often decided their ultimate fate in an arena where the horse was treated as royalty. As Cheyenne ended, Pete once again took to the road, heading for the next rodeo, and thinking of a girl in Arkansas.

That summer, a world-class rodeo was held in Chicago and Pete, who was competing in the bucking event in the windy city, once again met up with Babe. Having traded in his old Ford for a gleaming new two-door Chevrolet coupe, Pete telephoned Babe at her home in Arkansas, and asked her to meet him in Chicago. Unquestionably in love with him, she dropped everything and caught the first train north.

When Babe wasn't out at the rodeo grounds, cheering Pete on as he erupted from a chute on a rank, bucking bronc, she was walking hand-in-hand with him along Chicago's Lake Shore Drive, taking in the exotic sights to be found at Chicago's new Shedd Aquarium, and going out to dinner on Chicago's west side. Romance was in the air for the young couple, and a better place to nurture those feelings of love could not be found anywhere in America that summer. After the

Chicago Rodeo of 1931, the two lovers parted company with promises made that they were now 'boyfriend and girlfriend.' Pete drove on with Frank Sharp and Harry Knight to New York City and the Madison Square Gardens Rodeo, while Babe returned to her family home in Hot Springs.

The rodeo held at Burwell, Nebraska that year saw Pete Knight win money in the bucking horse event. Pete had arrived in the company of his two good friends and competitors, as a cloud of dust settled onto the blue coupe's hood in the field designated as a parking lot beside the Burwell arena. With fourth-place having been won and without further adieu, Pete drove out of Burwell as quickly as he had arrived, while Harry slept in the back seat and Frank studied the map and gave Pete his opinion on the best route to take – heading for the next big rodeo over the distant horizon – to eventually arrive on America's eastern seaboard. For days and nights, the boys drove on toward New York at high speed, passing solitary State Policemen in Iowa, Illinois, and Indiana. The uniformed troopers straddling big, dusty motorcycles often waved to them, but did not pull them over. Between spotting the trio of huge Stetsons and foreign license plates indicating the car's Alberta registry, officials hesitated to pull them over, and the car sped on.

New York's Rodeo was one of the four largest in North America, and as the name implied, cowboys and cowgirls represented all of the competing states and provinces across the continent. Pete Knight carried the banner for Alberta in the opening gala, and went on to win the World Series Bucking Championship.

Photo source: Harold Knight collection

Pete captured the bucking championship at Madison Square Gardens in October of that year, but only after the toughest competition was overcome. New York City's 'World Series Rodeo' was the last big bucking event of the season and was several days' drive from the western ranges dominated by familiar faces. Frank and Harry drove west with Pete as far as Indiana, and from there, they would entrain for Alberta. From Indianapolis – with trophies and prize-money and the record of his accomplishment in hand – Pete carefully laid his trophies and awards in the back seat of his Chevrolet coupé and set a course southbound down the narrow highways of America that would lead him by the most direct means to Hot Springs, Arkansas, and to the girl he had already promised his loving devotion.

For the rest of the autumn of 1931, Pete and Babe spent each day together, as he rested in the city of Hot Springs. Going to dinner with Babe at the city's grand old hotels, taking in a picture-show every week, attending endless gatherings at relatives' homes and soaking up the rejuvenating power of the hot mineral waters that this American city is famous for, Pete really got to know Babe Avant and the more he learned, the deeper his love grew. She shared his humor, laughed at the jokes he related from his many miles of travels, and learned of his likes and dislikes. His reciprocated love for Babe began to assume a sweet permanence of its own, as he courted his Arkansas beauty through the many weeks he stayed in Hot Springs. With the hankering to once again be moving, however, Pete kissed Babe goodbye, promising he would see her again in a few months.

Pete returned to Canada after the Christmas holiday of 1931, bunking with his brother Robert's family on their farm east of Crossfield. Every morning, Pete's seven-year-old nephew Raymond could hear his famous uncle waking in the next room. Pete awoke groaning for the first half-hour of every day, the result of more than a decade of muscular and structural abuse that was delivered to him on the backs and at times beneath the hooves of thousands of bucking horses on hundreds of rodeo infields. Waking each day was a searing, painful experience for the twenty-nine year-old bronc rider, and every morning he engaged in his own brand of stretching and calisthenics. He carried a home-made set of 'chest expanders' in his travelling bag, which he vigorously exercised with each morning. The expanders were nothing more than several springs and two wooden handles, which he would pull to their maximum tension several hundred times during each morning's workout. His upper body strength was unparalleled; the young athlete could reach above his head and suspend himself from a doorway moulding with the fingertips of one hand. Chinning himself with one arm, while working the muscles in the arm and shoulder, the bronc rider continued this for several minutes. Switching to the fingers of the other hand, Pete engaged in the same exercise with the other arm, over and over again, until he was satisfied with the exertion of the morning routine.

After he had taken his tortured body through nearly an hour of exercise, he hauled out his valet safety razor, sharpened it with the leather strop he carried in his bag and carefully shaved the hot lather from his face, often with his curious young nephew silently watching from the doorway. The day continued with breakfast, and after the meal, the men talked amongst themselves about the depression and the price of grain and cattle, while the young boys sat wide-eyed nearby and listened to every word, careful not to interrupt. Pete was as good an uncle as any young boy could have wished for, even aside from being famous. He would accompany his nephews out to the corrals or out to the pastures, talking about horses and farming, and always inquiring about what they were doing, always a good listener. Some days – with neighboring cowboys of Pete's age arriving at the farm to visit – all of the furniture was carried out of the farm home so that wrestling matches, twisting of wrists and a variety of other rough sports could be staged in the living room, with Pete taking on all comers. There was no liquor involved at these gatherings, nor did there need to be. Always, discussion would eventually come around to bucking horses and rodeos, and about the great cities that Pete had visited.

All of Robert Knight's older sons – Bobby, Peter, and Raymond – rode horses to school each morning, and all of these horses were little more than green-broke broncs. While Pete stayed with the family during his many visits, he accompanied the boys out to the main corral, assisted them in saddling up and then he would climb aboard and 'ride the rough' off the toughest horses. One named *Toppy* was the most notorious. *Toppy* was a wicked, ferocious bucking horse only at first light, and Pete took the horse lunging and bucking across the corral for more than a minute, until the pony settled down and was deemed fit for a schoolboy to ride that morning. One of these 'tame' horses in the Knight string was later sold to a neighbor; within a week the horse had killed the neighbor's hired man, after bucking him off and dragging him to his death on the open prairie.

In the spring of 1932 Pete once again left Crossfield and drove south, arriving in Texas in time to enter the Fort Worth Rodeo. Pete had called ahead to Babe, who met him at her sister's home in Fort Worth. With his mind finally made up, Pete knew he didn't want to be away from Babe if he could help it. He proposed to Babe that week, and she warmly accepted.

The Fort Worth Rodeo performances were indoor affairs, held at the Northside Coliseum. Built in 1908 and billed as the greatest marvel of architecture in the western hemisphere, the Coliseum dominated the centre of Fort Worth's stockyards district. The 1932 rodeo in Fort Worth was the first time a bucking horse event was ever aired to radio listeners. From a mobile NBC broadcasting station at centre infield, the performances of Pete Knight, Harry Knight, and John Jordan were followed by listeners in western Canada.

After the conclusion of one memorable evening performance of wild, hair-raising rides on bucking broncs, Pete, Babe, and Peggy, accompanied by John Jordan and Harry Knight, climbed into Jordan's big Chevrolet sedan and drove through the night to Hot Springs.

In the morning, Pete exchanged marriage vows with Babe before Justice of the Peace, Verne Ledherweed, while beaming witnesses looked on. When the ceremony was finished, the newly-weds and their entourage piled into the car for the return trip to Fort Worth: the bronc riding event had yet to be won and the boys remained in close competition against each other, a detail not to be interrupted by a wedding ceremony! Bleary-eyed and buoyed by the humor, camaraderie, and sober delight of the morning's events, the five travellers arrived back in the small Texas city that afternoon, where the three riders continued to accumulate points at the rodeo's evening performances.

After the Fort Worth Rodeo ended, Pete and his new bride started down the road together as a couple, heading for the first rodeos to be held in California that spring. Although Pete and Babe were leading a nomadic, ever-travelling existence, Pete's winnings

Pete and Babe Knight
After their first meeting in 1930, until their marriage in 1932, the young couple saw one another at every opportunity. Once married, the two were inseparable with Babe attending all the rodeos where Pete competed. No one would argue Babe was his biggest fan and strongest supporter.

Photo source:
Harold Knight
Collection

allowed them to live first class. They stayed in the best hotels that money could buy, wore the finest clothing and bought the latest model automobile – usually a Chevrolet coupé, as each year's new model rolled off the line – to carry them to the next rodeo event. When bankers or big-city business managers were earning fifteen hundred dollars in a year, Pete's annual income often topped seven thousand dollars.

The average rodeo contestants of the early 1930's and their wives were a thrifty, self-reliant, and tightly-knit group. Driving from one rodeo to the next across state and provincial lines or across an international boundary, the riders in those years looked out for each other along the way, in a never-ending extension of personal generosity. Although the Rodeo Association of America had come into being at Salinas, California, in 1929, the emphasis of this early association was on the protection of rodeo managers and the strictly-enforced adherence to management rules – on association saddles – by cowboy contestants.

During the stop that coincided with a rodeo, cowboys and their wives often lived in auto-camps or in third-rate hotels, cooked by the side of the road and washed out their own laundry as time would allow. It was a no-frills, nomadic existence fraught with chance and uncertainty. After a hard afternoon spent 'kicking out' bucking horses, whatever leisure the encampment enjoyed was usually little more than one of the cowboys strumming "The Red River Valley" or "My Swiss Moonlight Lullaby," on an old, travel-worn guitar. Pete and Babe had their fair share of such times, but like a lot of the top earners in the rodeo, Pete preferred to stay in finer establishments when they were available.

If a bronc rider received a minor injury that prevented further competition, the cowboys would pass the hat and collect a few dollars for him. If he was badly injured, the man would inevitably have a doctor's bill and worse, have no means to support himself or his family. There was no glamour associated with the living conditions reserved for a rodeo rider or his spouse, but if a contestant was good enough to win the day-money or the grand prize at a big rodeo, his expenses were covered for months after. It was a life where few contestants even attempted to take a wife on the road, and it was an era when a single woman could not easily endure the public opinion associated with travelling in the company of a bronc rider, unless she herself was a rodeo contestant in the barrel-racing event. There were only two dozen riders across the length and breadth of North America who were at the very top of their profession, and Pete Knight was foremost of that select group. Whatever the tribulations associated with the travelling, Babe was willing to endure them, and Pete was happy to make it as comfortable for her as possible.

On May 13, 1932, Pete entered the bucking horse contest in the California town of Livermore, an agricultural centre known for its lengthy growing season and world-famous wineries. Livermore was one of California's larger two-day rodeos; the first day of the event featured Pete riding as contestant number five and drawing a horse named *Black Serpent*. On the following day, Pete entered as contestant number forty-six and drew *Red Cross*, winning the rodeo's bucking horse event and the one hundred fifty dollar first prize; through it all, Babe cheered him on from the bleachers. Formidable riders from across the U.S.A. – Eddie Woods, Chuck Wilson, and Gene Ross – followed Pete's victory in the bucking horse event. *The Livermore Herald* declared a supplementary prize of five pairs of Levi-Strauss overalls to be awarded to the top bronc rider, donated by the town's foremost men's outfitter. Although most working men wore bib-overalls, Pete always dressed in gabardine western-cut dress trousers and matching shirts, with the added touch of a wide tie commonly favored by a banker or businessmen. The overalls, along with many of the bridles, saddles, and award-winning chaps, became gifted items that Pete gave away to friends and other people he admired. The unsung mechanics who worked on Pete's autos received the overalls – an added reward for keeping the legendary bronc rider's coupés 'mobile.' Pete sped through tens of thousands of miles every year. His cars were constantly receiving tune-ups, front-end alignments, grease-jobs, oil changes, and new tires for hard use on the highways of North America that Pete travelled to arrive in time to enter in the next rodeo.

9

Titles and Trophies

The former World Heavyweight Boxing Champion, Jack Dempsey and a great fan of rodeo, sponsored an event that was billed as 'The Ride of Champions' at Reno, Nevada, in June 1932. Dempsey donated a trophy, to be awarded to the champion bronc rider who could ride one of two featured 'unridable' horses in the event, in a qualified ride according to Cheyenne rules. It was intended to be the premier bucking event in all of the United States that summer.

The 1931 winners of the four biggest rodeos across North America were chosen to compete in this exclusive Nevada contest. Pete Knight, after winning in New York City, Earl Thode having won at Cheyenne, Gene Ross after capturing the North American Championship at the Calgary Stampede, and Frank Studnick having won the bucking event at the Pendleton Round-up, were all invited to Reno for 'The Ride of Champions.' It was an event that would decide who the best rider in North America was. The Dempsey Trophy carried far more acknowledged prestige in the United States than the Prince of Wales Cup. The Prince's Cup, after all, was not open to American bronc riders competing in Canada, and was relegated to a position of unimportance to bronc riders in or from the United States.

The Ride of Champions bucking event coincided with Reno's 'Pony Express Days,' beginning on Friday, June 24, 1932. Whoever won the Reno event, was entitled to keep the Dempsey Trophy outright. The contest was publicized in cities across North America and thousands of spectators arrived in Reno to witness the star attraction of the three-day bucking extravaganza. Reno's rodeo organizers had even written a song for contestants and celebrants to sing, played to the tune of the 1909 Heath & O'Donnell classic entitled "My Pony Boy."

In addition to the Dempsey trophy, four thousand dollars in cash prizes were offered, along with a championship award-winning saddle, and several gold belt-buckles, donated by Hollywood writer, John McCabe.

The four cowboys selected for the premier event had to prove their skills on one of two horses, both owned in part by Pete's good friend, Hayward stock contractor Harry Rowell. One horse carried the name of *Cannonball* and the other was a huge black stallion known as *Steamboat*. This horse was not the legendary

Steamboat of an earlier Wyoming, which would in time epitomize the great state with the horse's silhouette on the auto license plate. 'Cuff' Burrell, a well-known California bronc rider and stock contractor, introduced *Cannonball* and *Steamboat* to the Reno event. With neither horse having a known bucking history other than both being labeled 'unridable,' the outcome of the contest was heavily laden with speculation and wagers from the very beginning.

The official opening of the Pony Express Days was presided over by the California and Nevada Governors James Rolph Jr. and Fred Balzar, and Nevada's Lieutenant Governor, Morley Griswold, who led the grand opening parade on horseback through the streets of Reno in a mile-long spectacle of horses and riders. On the first afternoon of the rodeo's contested events, Friday, 24 June, 1932, more than two hundred cowboy and cowgirl competitors rode, roped, and bulldogged their way to victory or defeat, as the applause of the crowd spurred the contestants on. In the open bucking horse event, Idaho's Pat Woods won first place day-money, closely followed by Pete Knight – who had drawn a horse named *Bob White* –- and by Arizona's John Jordan. That Friday afternoon, Earl Thode drew *Man o' War*, while Frank Studnick 'kicked out' a bronc named *Troubles*. He spurred above the break of the shoulder on the first leap from the chute, and repeatedly spurred until the end of the ride, but despite his efforts, neither of the two award-winning cowboys managed to place in the day-money.

On the following day, the ride-off for the Dempsey trophy began, and the four invited champions prepared themselves for the premier event. The first contestant to ride was Gene Ross, who drew *Steamboat's* name from the hat. As the chute gate wheeled open on its oiled hinges, the horse charged into the infield, with Ross frantically hanging onto his buck-rein. On the third jump, the rider was unceremoniously thrown from the saddle and *Steamboat* claimed his first victim. When the applause subsided, a murmur went through the crowd as the next contestant prepared to saddle the horse he had drawn. All four riders carried reputations that preceded them across the west, and a collective question began to roll through the crowd: "Will anyone be able to ride these horses?"

Pete Knight had drawn *Cannonball.* Horse and rider erupted from the chute in a spinning, twisting whirl of white mane, tail hair, and flashing spurs. With Pete's balance steadied between his clenched fist on the buck-rein, his free clenched hand held high in the air, and his spurs slashing down each side of the bronc, *Cannonball* had no idea what had hit him. Every leap brought on a counter-stroke of hot, raking spur-rowels, as the horse did his best to lose his rider. By the seventh second, with all of the strength he could muster, *Cannonball* was flying high across the infield, twisting again and again, determined to buck Pete off – but to no avail.

The young Alberta cowboy, listed by local reporters as riding for Calgary, had made a qualified, winning ride on the previously unridable horse. On the eleventh second, Pete spurred *Cannonball* to a standstill before a cheering crowd of five thousand spectators. With the contest half-over, and the event's organizers allowing the two horses to rest for twenty-four hours before resuming, spectators and cowboys anticipated the next day's rides, regaling others late into the night with the display of horsemanship they had witnessed that afternoon. On the following day, the Ride of Champions event resumed. Earl Thode – who had accompanied Pete as a fellow competitor in the Alberta Stampede Company for three years, and had won the acclaim of thousands of fans at hundreds of rodeos – drew *Cannonball* for his ride in the contest. The horse had as much energy, stamina, and willingness to buck as he had on the previous afternoon. As Thode left the chute, the horse gave his rider the identical treatment the crowd had witnessed on the day prior with Pete in the saddle. *Cannonball* was more than a handful, however, and Earl Thode was quickly bucked off into the infield dust. The same fate awaited Frank Studnick on the horse called *Steamboat*. The bronc charged out of the chute, sending his young rider flying from the saddle, not five minutes after Thode had been bucked off his horse.

On June 26, 1932, the Dempsey Trophy was presented to Pete with unanimous approval, and the prestigious award became his to keep. As the photos were being snapped of Pete receiving the trophy from Nevada's Lieutenant Governor Griswold, and the legendary boxer, Dempsey, shook Pete's hand, Babe came forward to stand by her beaming husband. Pete held the trophy in one arm and his wife beneath his other, as the last flashbulb popped its brilliance, and the crowd roared its approval to the man who had become the greatest rider on the continent.

After an evening and a day of celebration with friends and competitors, Pete and Babe packed their bags, Pete's winnings, and the gleaming trophy, and departed Reno. Pete guided their coupé northeast on route eighty – with Babe leading him in her improvised rendition of "Pony Days" – as the happy couple headed across the state to Winnemucca and Elko, over the mountain ranges and across the state line to Salt Lake City, Utah. From Salt Lake City, the newly-weds headed north to Alberta.

Winning the Dempsey Trophy coincided with another 'first' for Pete Knight. That summer, after the Ride of Champions had concluded, Pete was declared

'World Champion Bronc Rider' for that year, in a unanimous vote made by the Rodeo Association of America (RAA), then based in Salinas, California. With the title, the RAA awarded Pete a five hundred dollar saddle, along with a five hundred dollar cash award.

On a long road that had begun in a farmer's wheat field in 1918, Pete had finally achieved what few other riders ever would, the title of the top bucking-horse rider in the world. It was because of Pete's typical modesty that Babe first learned of her famous husband's award, first from Harry Knight and then from a half-dozen other well-known bronc riders. All accounts were confirmed by newspaper reports. When she asked Pete about the World Champion title, he beamed his broad, quiet smile at her but said nothing. What was a title compared to holding Babe in his arms? His contentment in their love for one another held greater importance than any trophy or championship title.

The 1932 Calgary Stampede saw Pete riding at the top of his class, in a contest where bronc riders knew they had to ride for their lives to win against the already world-famous Pete Knight. After capturing the Dempsey Trophy, the World Champion title and a short list of other championships across the United States in the early summer of 1932, the acclaimed Crossfield cowboy entered the bucking competition in Calgary. Local reporters took a keen interest in Pete's entry to that summer's stampede. Predictions printed on the front pages of Calgary's *Daily Herald* and *The Albertan* all speculated on how their champion might fare in the bucking competition. Public curiosity drove the sale of newspapers to instantly greater volume.

It was a time for Babe to get acquainted to Pete's family, and her new in-laws did all they could to make her feel welcome. The couple spent many hours visiting with the two families, travelling back and forth between the brothers' homes east of Crossfield, and to other relatives' homes further east, in Beisecker and Irricana. With the Calgary Stampede finally beginning in the week ahead, Pete and Babe ended their visit to Crossfield and took a room at Calgary's Palliser Hotel.

In the first two days of the elimination rides, the stampede's bucking events moved along swiftly and efficiently before a packed grandstand of cheering fans. As the horses came tumbling out of the chutes with their riders spurring them on, Pete calmly waited for his turn to ride, quietly assessing the riding skill of each cowboy, and every bronc's ability to shake his rider loose. Close friends of Pete's and a few unfamiliar faces leaned off the top rail of the infield chutes, all waiting for their turn to ride, waiting to test every ounce of their skill in a contest they hoped to win.

On the third day of the stampede, Pete drew an unknown horse named *Flaxen*, a horse without a known history and therefore a bronc free of speculation. Upon leaving the chute the horse exploded into a squealing frenzy of madly pitching gyrations that no one could have anticipated. Reporters described Pete's ride as bronc-riding perfection. It came as no surprise that Pete won the first day-money for that afternoon. On the following day, Pete drew *Alberta Kid* and the famous pair won Thursday's first day-money in the Canadian bucking event. Friday – the day the semi-final rides were played out in both bronc riding events before thousands of spectators – was an afternoon described as a close-run-melee with bronc riders pulling down identical scores. That Friday afternoon, Pete won second day-money behind Harry Knight in the Canadian event. In the afternoon's North American event, Pete tied with Hub Whiteman, Sykes Robinson, and Turk Greenough for third and fourth day-money, behind the brilliant performances of John Jordan and Earl Thode, who had tied for first and second position.

That night, the annual cowboy ball was held in the lobby and ballroom of the Palliser Hotel. Although the party was anticipated with much enthusiasm every year, this year's event was the first time a 'live' music broadcast was featured for the benefit of radio listeners across southern Alberta, on Calgary's new CFAC radio station. Favorite western tunes were played and sung by Pete's good friends, 'Powder River' Jack and Kitty Lee on guitar and banjo, for a thousand party-goers

"Four Real Cowboys"
Calgary Stampede, 1932

From left to right: bronc rider, Harry Knight; musicians Kitty Lee and 'Powder River' Jack Lee; and Pete Knight

Photo source: Glenbow Archives

decked out in fashionable western wear, boots, and Stetsons. That night, Pete and Babe danced across the floor of the Palliser's ballroom, as their friends joined in the merriment that lasted until dawn.

Saturday was the last day of the stampede. With contestants and spectators still heavy-headed from lack of sleep – and in a few instances, an excess of liquor – the finals in the bronc riding events were battled out that afternoon.

The competition for the North American event had narrowed to two riders: Pete Knight of Crossfield, in competition with John Jordan of Prescott, also billed as the 'Arizona Kid.' The two riders tied for first place, and the tension began to mount. A ride-off would be necessary, for the two riders to break the deadlock. On Jordan's nod to the chute-man, the gate swung open and *Hornet* carried the Arizona Kid on a strong lead, bucking into centre infield. By the fifth second, however, Jordan was losing his balance. Snapping around to his left, *Hornet* dumped his rider in the seventh second, then swung back and savagely kicked the Arizona Kid in the face with a flying hoof. Getting up and then falling, Jordan stumbled back toward the chutes – blinded by his own blood – as cowboys ran onto the field to assist the rider. John Jordan was carried away to hospital in serious condition, and it was then Pete's turn to ride.

Pete had drawn *Slim the Swede*, noted to be one of the better buckers of that year's stampede. The horse bolted from the chute as the gate opened, kicking and bucking as Pete spurred him on. After the third leap, *Slim the Swede* went 'over the top,' rolling over Pete and tumbling in a heap of flying hooves and stirrups and dust. As the horse crashed onto the infield, Pete skidded out from under him, regaining his own feet before the horse recovered beside the pick-up horse. Pete came through the wreck unscathed, casting a quick smile up to where Babe sat as he strode back to the chutes, her initial concern still etched across her pretty features. After a momentary delay, the judges granted Pete a re-ride.

It took a few minutes to drive the shaking horse back around the corrals and into the chutes. With a practiced, fluid motion, Pete scrambled up the side of the railings and dropped down onto the horse's back. A quick nod from Pete, and *Slim the Swede* and his rider were again released from the chute, as the anxiety of the crowd reached a plateau. Pete never let up spurring the wildly bucking horse from shoulder to flank, his unique, cyclic spur-motion raking the rank palomino to a qualified, winning ride. The ten-second gun fired, the pick-up man rode into position, and Pete swung away from the bucking fury and landed on the infield, running. The crowd roared their approval, applauding again and again with appreciation for the bronc rider's performance, as Pete quickly made his way back to the chutes, waving his Stetson to his admiring thousands.

The judges declared Pete the winner of the stampede and North American Champion for 1932. John Jordan took the runner-up position, Oklahoma's Gene Ross took third, and Sykes Robinson followed in fourth place.

In the Canadian Bucking event, Harry Knight, riding a wildly-pitching bronc named *Coffin Nail,* won the Prince of Wales Cup for the second time. By a margin of only a few points, Pete Knight won runner-up position behind Harry, followed by Sykes Robinson and Saskatchewan's Lloyd Myers.

All of these riders depended on their skill, strength, stamina, but also on equipment suppliers who, in time, became friends and associates. Remaining in the backstage limelight, the equipment providers to the stampede's events were unsung heroes who were usually unknown to the fans, but were never forgotten by the riders.

Pete had a great many friends in the rodeo world, but one of his best friends was Eneas McCormick, co-founder of Calgary's *Riley & McCormick Saddlery* and a Calgary Alderman of the 1930's. *Riley & McCormick Saddlery* opened its doors in 1901 and eventually grew to its largest holding of thirty-five stores in centres across western Canada, by the mid 1970's. Young Mary McCormick, who later inherited the business from her father, fondly remembered Pete Knight and how polite he was when visiting the McCormick's store. Rough, tough cowboys darkened the doorway on a daily basis at Riley & McCormick's, so the appearance of a quiet, gentlemanly yet formidable bronc rider who was revered as a 'living legend' was a breath of fresh air to the proprietor and his family. Pete was so admired by the McCormicks, and his suggestions offered for design of riding equipment so highly-respected, that 'Pete Knight Stampede Chapps' were featured as "necessary items of riding apparel" in the August, 1932 Riley & McCormick catalogue. The manufacture of Pete Knight Stampede Chapps continued for more than fifty years afterward. The design was tailored as a streamlined, 'cut-down' bat-wing chap, a favorite of bronc riders for generations.

Pete's favored saddles – those manufactured by Riley & McCormick – were hand-made from wood and leather, and crafted by Johnny Foss, one of the finest saddle-makers in western Canada. On Foss's saddles, Pete performed some of his most spectacular rides, the foremost trait of the saddle-maker's work being "endurance, in the face of brutal punishment."

It was the boots, however, that marked Pete's profession with the greatest distinction. Pete had begun custom-ordering his boots during his tenure with the Alberta Stampede Company, on a recommendation from Earl Thode. Pete Knight's riding boots were hand-made on a custom 'Black French Calf' order from the *Charles H. Hyer and Sons Boot Company* in Olathe, Kansas, a company that had been in operation since the mid-1870's. Pete ordered an average of two pairs per year. When he needed a new pair to be made up, he mailed his order with a bank draft to Olathe, where the maker had Pete's long, slim, size nine measurements on file. It took several weeks for the order to be assembled by hand, but boots ordered from Olathe were shipped free of charge to anywhere in North America.

The square-toed riding boots Pete wore daily – with the boot's smooth kid-glove leather vamp absent of stitching – were the finest that could be purchased anywhere on the continent. It took Pete a minute to pull his boots on each day, after which the soft vamp leather molded around his instep. At the end of the day, it took him several minutes and a bit of assistance to pull the molded boots off of his feet, the spur-marks on the heels attesting to a hundred recent battles with bucking horses.

As Calgary's 1932 stampede ended, Pete had again stirred his fans to tears, and had added another Championship to his long list of accomplishments. There were now two formidable bronc riders who had placed their names twice on the Prince's Cup, and both named Knight. Those in the rodeo world and the thousands of fans who idolized their favorite bronc riders were buzzing with apprehension and excitement. Speculation ran rife over who would claim the Prince of Wales Cup as his personal property, and the field of prospective candidates had narrowed considerably.

Pete's greatest challenger in Canada was his good friend, Harry Knight. In the United States, the greatest competition for American accolades came from Earl Thode. As the year continued and the challengers stepped forward, Pete's lead often appeared to be on unsteady ground, but his skill was improving with age and his fame was growing across the west, and beyond.

10
Moving Up and Onward

When the Calgary Stampede ended in July of 1932, Pete and Babe once again headed south to Wyoming, as the Frontier Days Rodeo was kicking off in Cheyenne. Even after having had two flat tires, and competing in several small rodeos along the way, the couple still managed to arrive in Cheyenne with plenty of time for Pete to pay his entry-fee to the bucking event.

On the first day of the contest, Idahoan Pat Woods, who had won Wyoming's Cody Stampede the previous week, drew *Midnight* and was thrown in just under five seconds. On the same day, Pete Knight took fourth-place day-money on a horse named *King Tut*, winning behind Leo Murray, Bob Askins, and Earl Thode. The following day's first-money went to Gene Ross, and the day after that, the contest day-money was captured by Earl Thode. The top riders were all familiar names to Pete.

On the following Friday afternoon, Pete drew a horse named *Sundown*, but upon leaving the chute, the horse refused to buck, tearing across the infield at a dead gallop. The re-ride Pete was granted knocked him squarely into the second-place day-money for the afternoon, as *Big Enough* carried the spurring bronc rider in a mad frenzy of pitching gyrations for the full ten-seconds and ended with the enthusiastic applause of the Cheyenne crowd.

Cheyenne's Saturday spectators cheered the final competitions in the bucking event, as Earl Thode spurred his way to victory. The young Arizona cowboy took Cheyenne's 1932 bucking championship for a third time, leaving Pete in the runner-up position after the Alberta cowboy delivered a world-class performance on the compact *Five minutes to Midnight*. With several hundred dollars added to his accumulated winnings thus far, Pete and Babe said goodbye to their many friends in Cheyenne, and again hit the rodeo trail.

The three-day Pendleton Round-up World Championship Rodeo began on September 8, 1932. Once again, the premier riding talent of North America battled for laurels in a contest where the best bucking stock in the United States was featured. The Union Pacific Railroad offered specialty rates of five dollars for round-trip fares to Pendleton from the city of Portland, while spectators from as far away as Connecticut and the eastern Canadian provinces were registered at Pendleton's few hotels. Photographs of the riding events were rushed to Portland's *Oregonian* offices by an Army observation aircraft piloted by a Lieutenant Bond, and the events of the rodeo were not relegated to the sports pages of the newspaper, but enjoyed front-page centre-column status in the September 11 edition.

The cowboy contestants rode or sauntered across the infield and behind the chutes, wearing gaudy silk shirts with their contestant numbers pinned to the backs, while Round-up officials strutted through the infield marshalling pens and chutes with rodeo programs shoved into boots, in a fashion reminiscent of motorcycle policemen carrying their inevitable ticket-books. As in every other western locale that featured a rodeo or stampede, Pendleton rejoiced in the financial success of the three-day rodeo, the depression now hanging heavy in its third year.

When the horses were bucked out and the points tallied, the judges declared Pete Knight the winner of the bucking event. Pete had drawn good horses and had given each the best of his spurring technique, carrying away the Pendleton Championship for 1932.

With the completion of the Pendleton Round-up, Pete and Babe spent several weeks travelling from one rodeo to the next, sight-seeing in Washington and Oregon, and visiting friends along the way. The happy couple attended a rodeo held at the Oregon State Fair in Salem on October 1, and two weeks after that, the 'McCarty and Elliott World-famous Rodeo' opened, coinciding with the annual 'Pacific International Livestock Exposition' on October 15, in Portland. It was the first time that a rodeo had ever been featured at the prestigious Portland 'fat stock' show, and the horses McCarty and Elliott supplied for the eight-day indoor event were more famous than the cowboys who rode them.

Midnight topped the featured list, followed by *Big Enough, Satan, Golden Rule, King Tut, Five Minutes to Midnight* and a horse of added infamy, *Invalid*. The 22-year-old *Invalid* was described as 'picturesque' in his ability to throw all comers into the dust, with ease. From 1926 through '28, not one cowboy had mastered *Invalid* to a qualified ride, despite over one hundred and sixty attempts by some of the best riders in the country, including Pete. With top billing of wild broncs such as these being promulgated across the state, Oregonians thronged to the first indoor rodeo ever held west of Denver.

The first day of the contest was charitably declared children's day, and nearly five thousand spectators attended the first matinee performance. Cowboys from Pendleton, Cheyenne, Calgary, and hundreds of other locales across North America, gave the opening-day crowd more value than the fifty-cent admission promised. If Saturday's afternoon and evening performances were any indication of the interest displayed by the residents of Portland, the packed stands at Portland's Sunday rodeo were enough to confirm the wild enthusiasm.

Homer Ward of New Mexico was thrown hard, with a resulting fractured arm sending the young cowboy to hospital. In that evening's performance, Donald Nesbitt rode *Country Butter* to a third-place finish, following Cecil Henley who took second-place on *Broken Box*. Even in Portland, Pete Knight was famous to many, and as his name was announced, a cheer and a wave of unbroken applause went up from the crowd. As Pete left the chute on the Wyoming horse named *Golden Rule* and bucked him to a spirited ten-second finish, it came as no surprise to anyone that he won the Saturday evening's bucking event.

Pete came close to being eliminated from the contest, after drawing *Five Minutes to Midnight* on the afternoon of October 19 and battling the ferocious bronc in a ride that resulted in Pete being disqualified – again, after losing a stirrup. Babe sat in the stands and cheered her hero on, as the crowd gave the young Alberta cowboy a hand for his spectacular but failed effort. By that evening, however, Pete was back on the favored list to win in the overall competition, after delivering to four thousand Portland spectators what was described as a "thrilling exhibition" on the back of a horse named *Scarneck*. The evening's win secured another fifty points to his overall standing and assured his place in the competition for the big money at rodeo's end.

As the whirlwind of shows continued each afternoon and evening, the injuries sustained by the cowboy contestants began to mount. Three of the rodeo's riders were carried from the infield on stretchers, one of whom was unconscious, suffering a concussion, and a fourth cowboy managed to limp to the stadium infirmary unassisted. That same evening, Pete won third-place, after riding a horse named *Cross O'Baldy* in a balanced, qualified ride.

By Saturday, October 22, the four best bronc riders of the rodeo were declared on front page headlines: Alvin Gordon, Guy Cash, Oral Zumwalt, and Pete Knight. Highly impressed with the spectator response to the cowboys, *Oregonian* staff writer Lawrence Barber wrote, "the rodeo is the most popular entertainment seen by the citizens of Portland in recent years."

When the contest ended that night, Gordon was declared the winner, with Pete Knight winning the runner-up position and Guy Cash of Idaho taking third-place. In an awards ceremony following the announcement of the winners, the

Pacific Exposition committee for 1932 publicly expressed its heartfelt gratitude to the McCarty and Elliott Rodeo, for several reasons. Not only had the rodeo been the first of its kind ever produced in Portland, but for the first time in many years the exposition had finally paid off its debts and landed 'in the black.' For the citizens of Portland, the bucking horses and cowboys would be long remembered.

The highways of the United States and western Canada were home to Pete. When he wasn't waiting for his contestant's number to be called in Pendleton, Cheyenne, or some other city or town, he, along with Babe and often several other cowboys, were on the road. On hot days, the only air conditioning in the car was a window rolled down, and after days of travelling, the atmosphere and odors in the vehicle were positively rank. While Pete and Babe rented a hotel room enroute to a rodeo, the cowboys along for the ride would often sleep on the coupés comfortable, overstuffed seats – thereby saving half a dollar – where lingering odors from unwashed bodies permeated the car's upholstery.

No matter where he went, Pete seemed to know the best places to buy tires or have his cars serviced by the best mechanics in a given region. He drove his cars as he rode bucking horses – hard, and as fast as they would go. Pete rarely missed a rodeo, and it seemed there were usually two or three contests going on in the direction he was headed, all on the same day or at least a few days apart. Cowboys wearing dusty Stetsons, pungent-smelling levis and western shirts, piled out of Pete's car at each stop, descending on General mercantiles or small city supermarkets to buy the best but cheapest food they could for the long trip ahead. Grocers accustomed to carrying their customers on credit were often astounded to see a rumpled group of bewhiskered young men – all proudly wearing expensive, custom-made riding boots, with pant-legs tucked into the tops – pulling flattened rolls of five dollar bills from the inner bands of their Stetsons and leaving with small sacks of cooked beef and biscuits. Pete taught Babe to drive the coupé, and without the necessity of having a driver's license or vehicle insurance, she would often drive for hours while Pete slept. Often, one of the boys would spell Pete off at the wheel, as other occupants took turns driving, while the others talked or slept. With the car's trunk loaded to capacity with saddles and personal bags, several spare tires were tied to the trunk lid or onto the fenders of the car, and could be changed on the road and inflated with the car's hand pump, as was often required. On a main route between two large centres, automobile camps could be found along the way, inevitably patronized by cowboys heading in the same direction, to the same rodeo. Pete and Babe – with whomever was along at the time – always found friends and invitations to supper, during these isolated stops. If a cowboy needed anything along the way, help could always be found from other travelling cowboys.

Contestants shared the news of rodeos with other cowboys, and the hood of a 1929 Model 'A' Ford or a '32 Chevrolet coupé, served as a desk-top. With worn maps spread across the hood, groups of cowboys discussed the best routes to follow and what services to expect enroute. Someone was sure to have a copy of the latest *Hoofs and Horns* magazine, to check the dates of up and coming rodeos.

Pete was the generous source of many other cowboy's grubstake. Once, when Pete was entertaining his brother Walt and nephew Harold in a room at the Palliser Hotel, a knock came at the door. There stood a cowboy, looking red-faced, a bit bashful, and hoping for the loan of five dollars – just enough for food, a means to travel to the next event, and the entry fee. Without hesitation, Pete handed the cash to the stranger, who thanked Pete and left. Within an hour, two more cowboys arrived at Pete's door, each looking for financial help. With a hint of concern, Walt asked his brother why he was giving money to men he hardly knew.

"There wouldn't be a rodeo without contestants," Pete said with a shrug, "and no one else will provide for them."

Pete's generosity was legendary, and in Babe's own words, Pete never left his fellow cowboys empty handed. Although most of the cowboys were often far from home, they knew they could depend on Pete to get them out of a tough spot. After collecting his winnings at Madison Square Gardens at the end of the 1932 rodeo season, Pete loaded two of the show's injured cowboys into the back seat of his car and advised several other injured contestants to make their way to Hot Springs, by whatever means they could. Pete and Babe took the boys to Babe's hometown in Arkansas, where Pete rented a house for a half dozen injured riders, fed them, and aided in their healing. By the time the Denver indoor rodeo kicked off the 1933 rodeo season, all were fit to enter.

Not all who benefited from Pete's kindness and generosity were honest about it. One evening in Cheyenne, while Pete was checking into a hotel, the management presented the surprised cowboy with a bill for 'back-rent.' Someone had checked into the hotel a year earlier, signing the register in Pete's name. The lodger had skipped town, leaving an unpaid bill and a manager who knew of the famous cowboy. Although this was Pete's first visit to the hotel, in a silent acceptance that was typical of him, Pete paid the bill, and then rented a room for himself.

Pete was not a drinking man or an avid smoker, but there was a vice he pursued that he could not tear himself away from, and that was chocolate. While riding from one rodeo to the next, Pete munched his way through loads of the confection and replenished his 'sweets-larder' at grocery stores along the way.

With his beautiful wife, ownership of a farm in Canada, thousands of dollars in savings, a new car, a back seat full of good friends, and a sack full of chocolate under the seat, life could not have looked sweeter for Pete Knight. His life in the rodeo was carrying him to new heights and new experiences on a journey that would bring him untold fame and fortune.

11
A King's Ransom for a Rising Star

In July of 1933, the Rodeo Association of America declared Pete Knight the "World's Champion Bucking Horse Rider" for the second time. The Alberta champion had accumulated the highest point score over every other rider in the world, and received the accolade in his usual polite, quiet manner. To further honor this achievement, Pete was chosen to 'kick out' the first bucking bronc at the Chicago World's Fair Rodeo, which would begin in August of that year. The news of his ascendancy to World Champion Bronc rider for the second year in a row, found Pete and Babe in the hills behind Hollywood, where Pete was 'riding for the pictures.'

With the acclaim Pete received across the western United States, it wasn't long before his name came to the attention of silver-screen cowboy movie star, Tom Mix. Pete and Tom met at a California rodeo, and in time became good friends. Movie star and bronc rider each had considerable respect for the other's talents and accomplishments. Mix had become an experienced rider and rodeo contestant in Wild West shows at the beginning of the century, after leaving his native Pennsylvania. At the height of his career, Mix was earning an estimated seventeen thousand dollars per week, while producing and starring in 'cowboy' pictures, and this in a time when the cost of admission to a movie was less than a quarter. Tom invited Pete to appear for a screen-test, and the Alberta cowboy kicked out a string of the toughest broncs the studio could find for the producers in Burbank. The filmmakers of these early talking-films were ecstatic with Pete's talent, and polished ability on a rank bronc. As an enticement to remain in Hollywood and ride for the movies, one of Mix's producers offered Pete and Babe a villa in the Hollywood hills with seventy-five acres, an annual contract in motion pictures, and a substantial salary.

The money and additional perks had been strong enough enticements to sway him to do the screen-tests, but Pete turned the offer down. He was not a movie star, he explained, and didn't want anyone's head filled with notions of him as 'make believe,' or in any way damage the reputation of the rodeo in a confusing facsimile. No matter how true-to-life a movie might be, it wasn't real life, and could never be. Pete Knight was a Bronc Rider of the First Order. It didn't matter how much he was being offered to make movies, he simply did not see a future for himself riding 'docile' Hollywood horses in one predictable scene after another. With Babe fully supporting his decision, Pete politely but firmly declined the offer, leaving Hollywood and looking for the next world-class bucking horse contest; which at the time, happened to be in Calgary.

As Calgary prepared for a week of death-defying western competition at Victoria Park, the 1933 stampede began with great speculation by cowboys, reporters and thousands of ardent rodeo fans. The local press made much of the 'Pete Knight-Earl Thode' contest, described at the time as being one of the greatest riding battles in history.

Pete drew a horse named *Paleface* for his elimination ride, and Earl Thode drew a horse called *Diamond*. While Thode failed to score points on the second day of the contest, Pete delivered a sensational performance that won him the day-money for the North American bucking event. *Paleface* had loosened Pete by the fifth jump, with daylight showing between cowboy and saddle; in a second and a half, the rider made a startling comeback, kicking his way firmly into the saddle in a super-human effort and spurring the horse to a well-qualified finish. In the grandstand, the fans stood and cheered Pete's ride with thunderous applause, as the 'come-back' they had all witnessed was a seldom-seen spectacle of unquestionably superb horsemanship. Harry Knight, who had drawn a big sorrel outlaw named *Good Enough*, had been disqualified from the North American bucking event the day before, after Harry was thrown clear over the horse's head on the fifth jump. Despite having suffered an elimination from the one bucking event, Harry remained Pete's closest competition in the Canadian bucking event, and the tension was mounting. Thousands of eager spectators knew that this might be the summer the Prince's Cup could become one of the riders' personal property.

By Wednesday, the competition for the Canadian bucking event was even more tightly-focused on the two Knights. Both Pete and Harry enjoyed a huge 'fan-following' from the crowd, and everyone knew there was not a thing that one cowboy would not do for the other, further lending to the popular belief that the two formidable riders were brothers.

Harry drew a horse named *Sweet Murder*, while Pete drew *Bragg Creek Star*. Both riders kicked out their broncs – one after the other – and both riders made balanced, qualified rides, thereby assuring their positions for the contest to come.

By the fifth day of the stampede, twelve cowboys from Canada and twelve from the United States were battling each other in the semi-finals for the North American bucking event. By Friday evening, the contest had narrowed to twenty-one riders. In the Canadian event, fifteen cowboys qualified for the final con-

Pete Knight on Bragg Creek Star
Calgary Stampede, 1933
Photo source: Glenbow Archives

test, and speculation and informal bets made on who would win the two events peaked to a fever pitch.

In the Friday semi-final rides in the North American event, Pete Knight and his old friend Cecil Henley shared the first day-money in the contest. Pete and Cecil would be top contenders in Saturday's championship rides for the North American event, but everybody's focus was on the Canadian event, and the winning of the Prince's Cup.

In Friday afternoon's Canadian bucking event, Norman Edge took the first-place day-money, followed by Harley Walsh of Saskatchewan, with Pete Knight, Frank Sharp, and Herman Linder all tied for third-place day-money. It was an unexpected turn of events, but Harry Knight remained in the running for the one event, and Pete's performance was delivered that day in his strong, confident style. As revelers attended the cowboy ball at the Palliser that night, all discussion – amid the swirl of dancers, fiddle-music and drinking – seemed to revolve around the Prince of Wales Cup.

Saturday afternoon – the final day of the stampede – found the Victoria Park grandstand packed to capacity, as the bucking contest began before a crowd of over twenty thousand spectators. Cowboys and farmers had driven in from ranches and farms more than three hundred miles from Calgary, just to pay for a place to stand in front of the grandstand that afternoon to see who would win the Canadian championship.

Of the two bucking contests, the North American event was played out first. As one rank bronc after another left the chutes, a dozen cowboys with aspirations of winning the North American championship were knocked out of the competition, all either failing to stay in the saddle or suffering disqualification.

Pete's name was announced, and he made his way up onto the chutes, easing gently down onto his saddled bronc. Pete had drawn the horse, *Satan*, and as the chute swung open, both horse and rider emerged in a pitching battle that had the crowd breathless with anticipation. Spurring his way into a balanced, roiling melee, Pete rode the tough, wildly-bucking *Satan* to a winning spur-driven ride, the applause carrying across the infield for a long, unabated moment when the ten-second gun fired and the battle had ended. It was clear that Pete stood a good chance of winning the event, but it was time for the Canadian Bucking event to be fought out, and the crowd eagerly, and impatiently waited.

As the bucking event played out that afternoon, fifteen highly-experienced bronc riders – all battling to place their name on the cup – rode the bucking horses they had drawn out past the plane of the chutes, one after the other. Several were bucked off, two lost stirrups and in several more cases, the horses failed to put up a fight. Harry Knight's name was announced and the crowd applauded, every one of Harry's thousands of fans cheering, whistling and calling his name. Hundreds of Banff's residents were in Calgary for the stampede, to watch their hometown boy battle for the championship. As the chute swung open, Harry spurred a horse named *Thunder* into the first leap, and the tall, lanky bronc rider continued to rake the horse's shoulders and flanks with gleaming silver rowels. By the fourth leap, however, Harry was in trouble – *Thunder* upsetting his balance ever so slightly. Into the seventh second, *Thunder* knocked the young cowboy from Banff out of his spurring rhythm, and in the second after that, Harry was on the ground – bucked off and disqualified – as the horse leaped away from rider. With a faithful show of support for his effort, the grandstand crowd applauded Harry as he made his way back to the chutes, smiling at the supporters and waving his hat. Now, it was Pete Knight's turn for the final ride in the Canadian event.

Pete had drawn *Too Bad*, the same horse that had sent Harry flying from the saddle on the Monday prior. Pete gave his quick nod to the chute-man, and in a heartbeat, both bronc and rider were flying into centre infield. Pete had a previous relationship with this horse, and knew that *Too Bad* could be completely unpredictable. He was the same horse that had won the acclaim of 'toughest horse' in the 1928 stampede, the same year he had 'somersaulted' across the infield with Pete miraculously keeping his place in the saddle. With that in mind, Pete maintained an iron grip on the buck-rein, spurring the horse across the infield – straight up and then straight down, in a whirling, jarring frenzy – as the crack from the ten-second gun brought the grandstand crowd to a standing ovation, with hammering, thunderous applause.

When the points were added up by the judges, it was established that, for the second time, Pete Knight had achieved another astounding victory, winning *both* the North American and the Canadian bucking championships in a single afternoon, literally single-handed. The Prince of Wales Cup, that most prestigious award that had been dedicated by a future King of England only ten years before, was now the personal property of Pete Knight. The most noteworthy sporting award ever presented in Canadian history – designed, paid for, and gifted as a national treasure to Canada, by the heir to the British throne – would be his to keep for the rest of his life.

In the hours and days after the 1933 Calgary Stampede ended, life for Pete and Babe Knight was a seemingly-endless, surreal kaleidoscope of warm family gatherings, parties thrown in their honor by close friends, and well-wishers pouring out their heart-felt congratulations for Pete's accomplishment. Crossfield's citizens rejoiced over the success of their most celebrated hero. Keeping a room at the Palliser for more than a week after the stampede, the famous bronc rider and his beautiful wife were constantly surrounded by throngs of dignitaries and cowboys; the latter all beloved friends who had made their mark in the rodeo, and who firmly believed that the Prince's Cup had finally gone to the most deserving recipient of all.

With the winning of the Prince's Cup, Pete once again headed south to challenge all comers in the big rodeos below the border. In Cheyenne at the end of July, the bucking contest was fought out between Pete Knight and Earl Thode, each winning first day-money, in the first two days of the rodeo. When the points were tallied on the final day, however, Turk Greenough made the winning ride that summer in Cheyenne, and took the Frontier Days bucking championship for 1933. At the end of Cheyenne's 'exhibition ride' that summer, the legendary bucking horse *Midnight* was retired by his owners, McCarty and Elliott.

The solid silver trophy was commissioned in 1923 by the Prince of Wales (later becoming King Edward VIII of England). As the premier Canadian Championship Bucking Award, the trophy would be decreed as the property of any Canadian Bronc Rider who had placed his name upon the trophy three times.

Pete Knight won the Championship in 1927, 1930, and 1933.

Today the cup rests in the Pete Knight Memorial Showcase at the Cowboy Hall of Fame in Oklahoma City, USA.

Photo taken in 1927, upon Pete's first win of the prestigious award.

Photo source: Glenbow Archives

After the win, it was back on the road. Pete and Babe, with Harry Knight and Frank Sharp riding along in the back seat of a new maroon Chevrolet coupe Pete had bought the week before, all headed for Chicago. On the way to Illinois, Pete, Harry, and Frank made memorable bucking entries at the Sidney Rodeo in Iowa, as Babe cheered her heroic, formidable husband on from Sidney's small grandstand. Again, they took to the road, eastbound across the Mississippi River and into Illinois. Spectators would see many rodeos in the United States featuring Pete Knight in the competition, but the greatest contest of all that year was held in the city of Chicago.

The Chicago World's Fair Rodeo began on the Friday afternoon of August 25th, 1933, before an afternoon crowd of twenty-one thousand spectators. Pete was awarded the privilege of kicking-out the first bucking bronc of the contest at Soldier's Field Stadium, in a contest lauded by comedian and trick-roper Will Rogers as being the Olympic Games of western sports. The 'Cowboy Senator' from the great State of Arizona, James Minotto, was the rodeo's President, who successfully wooed Chicago's society in a pre-rodeo celebration at the city's prestigious Century Club. The rodeo was committed to honoring a Century of Progress, both in spirit and in fact, to counteract the crushing spectre of the depression hanging as a backdrop across the entire continent.

For seventeen days contestants from across western Canada, fifteen of the United States, and Mexico engaged in a daily competition and demonstration of their skills at riding, roping and bulldogging. The wild horse race event was featured in Chicago for the first time, that year. While a common event in many previous western rodeos, it was a first for the windy city. One hundred fifteen bucking horses and more than one thousand head of other livestock were sent to Chicago, for the western spectacle. One hundred twenty-five riders – all having a minimum five-year outstanding record in North American rodeo, and attending by special invitation only – were determined to make their mark, while riding the toughest and the meanest in a truly world-class event. Although the professional ability of the cowboys competing was above reproach, serious accidents mounted quickly soon after the rodeo events began. For some, performance jitters interfered with concentration. The prestige attached to eligibility for competing in the World's Fair contest and the pressure the contestants felt while giving their all as representatives of their home-towns, states, and provinces were intimidating factors for many. A trick-rider from Fort Worth fractured her left arm after falling from her galloping horse, requiring ambulance attendants to carry her to Chicago's St. Luke's Hospital. Other riders suffered scrapes, sprains, and bruises, but none came closer to losing his life than one of Alberta's most noteworthy contestants.

On the third day of the bucking horse event, Harry Knight was thrown and trampled by a horse named *Big Boy*, smashing Harry's pelvis and causing extensive internal injuries. A hush of anxious concern descended on spectators and contestants alike, as Harry was rushed from the field to a waiting ambulance. On arrival at St. Luke's Hospital, life-saving surgery was performed without delay on Harry, who remained in a coma for a day afterward. Idaho contestant, Jack Kerscher, donated blood to the young Alberta rider, through a person-to-person transfusion, and then returned to the rodeo that evening to win the bulldogging contest for the day, placing the best 'time' in the event for the entire week. When announcers declared Kerscher's win, and his life-giving contribution to Harry Knight, the crowd went wild with appreciation for the young Idahoan. From that day on, the cowboys were treated as royalty wherever they went in Chicago.

While Harry's condition slowly improved, Pete and Babe kept in constant and reassuring contact by telephone with the injured cowboy's mother, who anxiously waited for word of her son's health, at her home in Banff. Each day, after the bucking competition was finished for the afternoon, Harry's hospital room would fill with cowboys during the precious few visiting hours he was allowed. Pete had insisted that Harry have a private room, and paid for it out of his own pocket. He and Babe spent several hours of each day at the hospital, most of their time spent with Harry, but each day more riders were injured as the events were played out to the grandstand crowd.

'Shorty' Hill of New Mexico was injured by a Brahma steer and was also sent to hospital, followed shortly after by Francisco Aparcio from the Mexican Charro Troupe. Although Aparcio was an expert rider, his collar-bone was fractured after he fell from a wild horse he was attempting to mount, while transferring from his well-trained pony during a galloping pursuit.

Chicago's citizens and visitors had witnessed a week of spectacular rodeo competition, thrills, spills and injuries, when Senator James Minotto declared that a large percentage of the rodeo's proceeds would be donated to Chicago society's *Red, White and Blue Club* from the September 7 rodeo events. The club's benevolence assisted in feeding, clothing, and educating five hundred children per week in Chicago's poor neighborhoods, and all of Chicago's affluent society families contributed to the one-day event that placed hundreds of sorely-needed dollars into club coffers. In yet another act of charitable generosity that week, over five thousand underprivileged children from Chicago and surrounding areas were admitted to the rodeo free of charge. As large throngs of Chicago patrons gathered at Soldier's Field Stadium to see the display of western derring-do, Pete Knight took the leading point score accumulated in the bucking contest. It was a stunning achievement, after five days of eventful bronc-riding competition, and after winning Wednesday's and Thursday's day-money. For others, the injuries mounted.

By Thursday, August 31, eighteen contestants had sustained serious injuries in seven days of heated competition, with the nineteenth casualty that day being Idahoan bronc rider, Pete Grubb. The young rider was thrown heavily from the horse he had drawn, sustaining a concussion on impact. Grubb was carried unconscious to St. Luke's Hospital, to join an ever-increasing ward of badly-injured rodeo riders. 'Smoky' Snyder of Kimberley, British Columbia, was thrown and trampled by a Brahma bull, sustaining a fractured collarbone beneath the bull's onslaught. With Pete and many other riders passing through an inferno of close calls unscathed, the rodeo's events carried on unabated. Leonard Ward of Oakdale, California, won a Saturday afternoon bucking event, while Eddie Woods and Pete Knight tied for second and third-place day-money, and following hard on their heels were Eddie Curtis and Earvin Collins.

As the rodeo continued into its second week, President Roosevelt's son and daughter-in-law, Mr. And Mrs. James Roosevelt, made a grand entrance to Soldier's Field stadium astride dappled grey horses and were then installed in the best centre-field seats to view the rodeo's proceedings. James Roosevelt and his wife were introduced to several of the leading riders from each event, including Pete Knight.

A recently-injured Pete Grubb returned to Soldier's Field that afternoon, to make a startling comeback in a qualified ride that won him the day-money on Tuesday, September 5, against riders Alvin Gordon, Turk Greenough, Herman Linder and Hub Whiteman. Grubb's outstanding ride was another proof that life went on for an injured cowboy, and whether it was Pete Knight, or Harry, or one of their friends, riding bucking horses went hand-in-hand with injury.

To draw more spectators to the stadium, Senator Minotto authorized the shortening of the infield, thereby bringing the paying patrons closer to the action, and the price of admission was lowered to forty cents per ticket. As the charity rodeo of 7 September began that afternoon, Pete Knight continued his lead in the bucking horse event. He had achieved and maintained the highest point-score in the event, followed only by Earl Thode, who was several hundred points behind Pete.

On September 10, 1933, Chicago's *Sunday Tribune* reported that the two rodeo performances from Saturday had admitted over fifty thousand enthusiastic spectators to the afternoon and evening programs. Because of these numbers, the promoters announced their decision to extend the show for five days longer, announcing a new closing date of September fifteenth.

For the first time in two years, a cowboy finally made a qualified ride on *Five Minutes to Midnight*. Perry Ivory of Altura, California, had drawn *Little Five*. Kicking and bucking across Soldier's Field in a flurry of tail-hair, mane and dust, he managed to stay aboard the compact little horse for the required ten seconds. Four days later, Pete Knight also drew *Five Minutes to Midnight*, determined to master the horse, after Ivory's example. In a spectacular display of horsemanship, Pete rode *Little Five* to a stunning, bone-jarring qualified ride. Pete's performance was exceptional that evening, but Herman Linder of Cardston, Alberta, won the day-money for the event, followed by South Dakota's Melvin Tivis, Hub White-man, Turk Greenough and Alvin Gordon.

On the following day, the contestants participated in a Grand Parade through the streets of Chicago while thousands of Chicago urbanites and many more thousands of visitors lined the parade route to cheer the cowboys on. The conga-line of horses and riders snaked its way back to the stadium, as the clouds over Illinois gathered in preparation for a torrential downpour. Soldier's Field arena quickly became a quagmire. For two days, the steady rain ended all opportunity for the cowboys to add to their day-winnings, and kept fans from the stadium. The weather gave the contestants a much-needed rest from their rigors, and time to reflect on the grandeur of the show in which they had been chosen to participate.

The World's Fair Championship bucking contest ended after more than three weeks of grueling competition, with Pete Knight winning the event. The news of his victory was trumpeted across the west, particularly to Albertans from the front pages of Calgary's two competing newspapers and over the airwaves from Calgary's fledgling radio broadcaster. The World's Fair was the biggest, most prestigious show on the continent, and Pete's victory came as a feather in his home province's cap. In the halls of Alberta's Legislature, toasts were made to the province's cowboy hero, and his name became synonymous with the ability to win, in the face of all odds.

As the American anthem was played to the thousands of applauding spectators in the stadium, Pete received the awards for his victory from Senator Minotto, including one thousand dollars cash and a five hundred dollar trophy saddle.

Following the awards ceremony, the evening was spent at Harry Knight's bedside, as Pete and Babe did as much as they could to cheer their badly-injured friend. Doctors had advised that Harry might never walk again, and riding in competition would be out of the question. On the telephone to Harry's mother, Pete kept the worst news from her, providing glowing updates of her son's improvement. Without a doubt, he told her, Harry would have a speedy recovery and be up and around in no time. Leaving Harry was not easy, but Pete paid the medical bill owing, and assured the hospital's management that anything the young cowboy required would be paid for, including a first-class train ticket home to Banff, when he could be moved. Other cowboys came forward without having to be asked, providing cash not only for Harry Knight but for all of those cowboys injured, thereby ensuring that all medical assistance would be paid for.

From Chicago, the rodeo's contestants moved on to Indianapolis, where a two-week rodeo was featured, made even more popular across Indiana by press coverage given to Chicago's recent world-class event. When the Indianapolis Rodeo ended, the cowboys once again took to the highways and headed east to New York City for two weeks of rodeo competition in Madison Square Gardens. From the splendor and opulence of Wall Street, North America's renowned rodeo contestants took their winnings and moved on, to the first western rodeo ever to be held in the Boston Gardens. The Boston Rodeo – an indoor event – was the last big rodeo of the year. With the final anthem being played in Boston, and the awards being distributed, Pete and Babe once again headed down the highway to Arkansas, where Christmas would be spent with the Avant family.

The year had been the best of his life. With a year marred only by the near-death of his best friend, Pete had taken the rodeo world by storm. The winnings that he had accrued from months on the rodeo trail had accompanied a second official world-title, capturing the Prince of Wales Cup for his personal property, and taking the World's Fair title, as well. It was time to give himself and his lovely wife a well-needed rest, not knowing at the time that his fame was about to go beyond the shores of North America.

12

Bucking for International Acclaim

America's foremost travelling rodeo of the twentieth century was 'Tex' Austin's Cowboy Troupe. The show was famous around the world during the 1930's. In 1934, the Tex Austin Troupe was invited by the National Sporting Club of England to stage a month-long rodeo in London, and select cowboys from across the United States, Australia, and Canada were invited to compete in a contest and pageant to be held at London's massive White City Stadium. Pete Knight, Frank Sharp, Herman Linder, and seven other award-winning riders from western Canada were invited to compete before the British audience. Another twenty formidable American bronc riders and several Australian champions were included on the roster of this most prestigious display of western-style horsemanship. More than a hundred and fifty cowboys and cowgirls made up the show's riding and roping specialists, privileged to be included in such an extravagant affair, especially at the height of a depression.

Pete and Babe boarded the luxurious cruise-liner *Aurania* with a complement of cowboys and other passengers on the Montreal docks, while the other cowboys in the troupe took passage with the horses on the rough but durable steam-freighter *Nortonian*, bound for a Welsh port with the rodeo's bucking horses and other stock. Herman Linder worked his way across the United States on the troupe's special stock-train, feeding the horses enroute and cleaning out the stock-cars for the generous sum of five dollars per day, and free board on the train. McCarty and Elliott were the stock contractors commissioned to supply the horses and other livestock, with *Invalid* and *Five Minutes to Midnight* included in the troupe's top bucking string. *Midnight* was brought out of retirement – the legendary bucker having been royally-treated with his own barn and pasture in Wyoming – to make the special trip to the London Rodeo. Scores of other passable bucking horses were sent from the Wyoming foothills on the epic journey, as well.

When the *Aurania* set sail from Montreal for the ten-day cruise to England, the ship's passengers; the cowboys, and their wives and sweethearts among them, all joined in the merriment to create a festive spirit for the special occasion. Pete and Babe dined in first-class style, danced to the music played by a twelve-piece orchestra, and sipped champagne on the long voyage. Pete became accustomed to wearing a dinner jacket and politely participating in the dinner table conversation, while Babe, dressed in the latest New York fashions, and wearing a small string of real pearls, regaled the table's other guests with the feats her famous husband had performed on bucking horses. Pete would smile but say nothing, leaving the true tales that Babe related to their fellow travellers, sounding far-fetched to some.

The passengers were suddenly jarred from their merriment when the ship scraped upon a rocky escarpment off Cap du Sante, the ship's momentary 'running aground' causing perforations to several water-tight compartments in the vessel's hull. After a lengthy inspection performed at Quebec City, the ship was deemed safe to sail for England. Two days later, *Aurania* made her way beyond the St. Lawrence, leaving Canada behind for the open seas.

On the same day, *Nortonian* departed from her American port – the rolling, old steamship passing through coastal waters to arrive on the high, blue Atlantic. Prior to *Nortonian* setting sail, Frank Sharp was promoted to 'stock manager.' Frank oversaw the cleaning of stalls, and feeding and watering of livestock in a daily routine with two dozen other cowboys, as the *Nortonian* rode through jarring North Atlantic seas, on a course set for the city of Cardiff, Wales, in the United Kingdom.

After a highly-publicized disembarkation on the Cardiff docks, the troupe-members, escorting the rodeo's stock, located the trains that would carry the livestock, and made the two-day trip to London. The other contestants and their wives – having previously arrived on the faster *Aurania* and safely docked at Southampton after a voyage devoid of further mishap – were comfortably installed in a lavish tourist hotel near White City Stadium. By North American standards, the rooms were considerably smaller, but the décor, services, and hotel's restaurant menu was comparable to any five-star accommodation that could be found in New York or Chicago – a long climb from sleeping on coupé seats in auto-camps, as the cowboys were accustomed to.

Tex Austin's World Championship Rodeo began on Wednesday June 6, 1934, and was scheduled to perform daily until the second week of July.

The Directorship of England's Royal Society for the Prevention of Cruelty to Animals (RSPCA) was not enthusiastic about the appearance of a western rodeo in London, from the onset. 'Cowboy' pictures playing in English cinemas each week churned out images of rearing horses, shoot-outs between riders at a dead gallop, in what the RSPCA considered to be wanton misuse of horses for the sadistic pleasure of a viewing public. The movies left an indelible, unsavory stamp upon

British society. The actual name of the rodeo's premier activity was not to be referred to as 'Bronco busting,' but rather, 'Buck jumping.' Further restrictions were imposed by the RSPCA against pre-advertisement of the rodeo.

In a stadium designed for Olympic games with a seating capacity of over one hundred thousand, a mere three thousand spectators arrived for each day's performance. The promoters had serious doubts about the show's ultimate success. The consensus that the rodeo had been set upon by the RSPCA before the rodeo even arrived in England appeared all too real. A half-dozen inspectors representing the society hovered in the grandstand during each performance, their positions in the crowd strategically placed by RSPCA Chief Inspector, Thomas Finn, to ensure maximum coverage of every angle of the infield, while taking note and recording every comment made by nearby spectators. The society demanded that the calf-roping event be performed with a break-away string on each lariat; that the riders' spurs be completely wadded in tape; and that the flank-strap beneath the horse's belly be tied to within six inches of the saddle's cinch-strap. At any rodeo in North America, all of these constraints would have been laughable, then or now. Lariettes were designed to take the full weight of a young steer snapping at rope's end, the flank-strap was tight on the horse's flank, and the spur-rowels – while not sharpened – were free to spin on their tiny axles, gleaming in their mounts. News of the restrictions cast an immediate pall over the cowboys' spirits.

Meanwhile, the spectators of the White City Rodeo were making bets on the skills of Canadian cowboys versus their American counterparts. Reference to Pete's three-time victory, leading to permanent ownership of the Prince of Wales' Trophy at the Calgary Stampede, appeared in the *London Times*. The media had previously expressed enthusiasm for the rodeo from the start, referring to the grand entrance of the cowboys and cowgirls on the first day of the rodeo as "a living frieze . . . in a dream-like unending procession . . . of lofty Stetsons and gaily-colored shirts." Patrons were hushed in disbelief as the grand parade of cowboys and cowgirls – all mounted on western saddle horses – entered the stadium while a band announced their arrival. While the strains of John Phillip Sousa's "Beneath the Double Eagle" and Victor Herbert's "Irish Rhapsody" wafted across the stadium infield, many of the thousands of spectators were heard to whisper, "They really do exist!" and hundreds of British schoolchildren invited to attend the rodeo were thrilled to witness a spectacle most would never see again. Everyone cheered and applauded as the cowboys rode through the stadium on their grand entry parade route.

With the rodeo's organizers complying with the demands of the RSPCA, noted horses such as *Midnight* and *Five Minutes to Midnight* bucked with only half the enthusiasm and none of the spark normally exhibited for North American spectators.

When the schoolchildren were requested afterward by their teachers to write compositions reflecting their impressions, the only disappointment expressed by the students was that the cowboys weren't carrying six-shooters and that red Indians with feathers and bows and arrows were nowhere to be seen in the western pageant. It came as a surprise to teachers that the children were not aware of witnessing any act that could be deemed 'cruel,' in the rodeo's various events.

Babe Knight watched the show from her reserved seat at centre stadium, and while Pete rode the horse he drew in a clean exhibition of professional showmanship, Babe could clearly see his disappointment, in spite of his polite, gentlemanly manner. Several days after the rodeo began, Pete provided an interview to media personality, Lord Castlerosse, giving an honest, matter-of-fact description of the contest. When Lord Castlerosse asked Pete whether good bucking horses enabled a rider to win more points than a poor bucker, Pete confirmed it was true and then added,

"Of course, you've got to be able to ride your horse."

Pete's answer was an intentional double-entendre. Not only did a cowboy have to have the skill to retain his place in the saddle, but the rider must also be *allowed* to buck the horse by 'Cheyenne rules,' as had originally been dictated in rodeo contests across North America, from the inception of the bucking horse event.

As the rodeo played out through its first week, Tex announced that the rodeo's proceeds from Sunday, June Seventeenth, would be donated to several British hospitals, but organizers were shocked to learn an official protest against a Sunday performance had been lodged by England's 'Lord's Day Observance Society.' The society recruited the assistance of the Bishop of London, who publicly denounced Sunday performances in a letter to the *London Times* newspaper. In response to the Society's opposition, the National Sporting Club's director wrote letters to the hospitals earmarked for the rodeo's donation. He requested opinions from the management of the hospitals regarding the Observance Society's claims. Debate on the questions of morality and ethics of Sunday rodeos in London was fought out in the *Times* between the Bishop and the National Sporting Club, but the Bishop had already voiced his opinion.

The numbers of spectators arriving at White City dwindled for the Sunday charity performance, a testament to the enduring faith practiced by Britons. The National Sporting Club Organizers finally relented, and no rodeo events were conducted on Sundays for the remainder of the rodeo's performances.

Whereas the 'Lord's Day Observance Society' had only threatened legal action against the rodeo, the RSPCA pressed charges of animal cruelty against White City, Tex Austin, and roping contestant T.J. Richards, after a calf roped with a breakaway-rigged lariat ran through a wire fence during an afternoon performance. Richards was charged by prosecutors Jones and Cassels for 'terrorizing' the calf with his pursuing saddle pony on June 11, leading to the calf's destruction. At a West London Police Court hearing on Saturday, June 30, the charges against the rodeo were dismissed by Mr. W. J. H. Broderick and the three defendants received five guineas each – roughly thirty American dollars – from the RSPCA, for legal costs.

Without adequate numbers of spectators arriving through the turn-stiles to pay for the rodeo, Austin lost a fortune on the venture. Many patrons arrived at White City just to watch the more affordable dog-races. The winners of the rodeo events received their winnings, however, with the bucking horse title going to Alvin Gordon of Montana. Ownership of the best bucking horses of the rodeo was retained by McCarty and Elliott, while a hundred of the troupe's other horses and livestock were sold at auction. The black horses were the most sought after by horse-drawn funeral-hearse operators from London's outlying towns and boroughs. For Pete and Babe, the remainder of their holiday in England was happily spent as an extended overseas honeymoon, after being married for only two years. They travelled across the country, soaking up the history and the culture of a country neither had imagined they would ever see. Busloads of cowboys visited Buckingham Palace to witness 'The Changing of The Guard,' and Epsom Downs Derby to watch the horse races, from centre stage seats adjacent to the king's glassed-in box.

By 1932, the Knight family in North America had long since lost all contact with their relatives in Stockport, England, and it is likely that distant relatives living in the small English town were not even aware of their relationship to the famous bronc rider.

Other cowboys, like the injured Herman Linder, chose to head home at the rodeo's close. He left for Canada on an early sailing of the CPR liner *Empress of Britain*, and arrived in Canada in time to enter the contest at that summer's Calgary Stampede. Earl Thode, who had suffered a skull fracture at White City, also considered himself fit enough to travel home, but on a different sailing. Arriving in

Canada before the beginning of the 1934 Calgary Stampede, Thode returned to his in-law's home in Canmore, Alberta, for a well-deserved rest before the stampede began.

London's White City Rodeo was eventful and filled with strange sights for all of the rodeo's participants and their travelling companions, but the prospect of shipping a western rodeo to England was never again seriously contemplated by the organizers or contestants who rode at White City Stadium in the summer of 1934.

Tex later claimed he lost more than two hundred thousand dollars in the White City Rodeo 'fiasco' and emphatically told American reporters, "We're not going back."

Pete didn't compete at the Calgary Stampede during the drought-stricken summer of 1934. After completing their tour of England, Pete and Babe returned to Canada and travelled through the United States to Wyoming, for that year's Cheyenne contest.

Later that fall, Australian shores beckoned. With an invitation from Stewart McColl's Melbourne-based rodeo pageant, Pete and Babe eagerly made the voyage to Melbourne, Australia.

The Australian horses were smaller by North American standards, and weighed an average of nine hundred pounds – two hundred pounds less than most bucking horses found in Cheyenne or Calgary. American cowboys performing in the pageant included Pete's boyhood hero, Yakima Cannutt, Clay Carr, and Johnny Schneider. The riding event boasted Mexican ropers, mid-eastern Camel riders, and Czarist-Russian Cossacks. The show was warmly received, but many an afternoon's performance was cancelled, due to heavy rains falling on Australia's southern coast. Performing exhibition rides for an audience that appreciated great horsemanship, Pete was acclaimed by Australian fans, and expert horsemen alike, to be a true world's champion rider of "buck jumpers."

For Pete and Babe, the trip was a memorable visit to the land down under, and people everywhere in the Australian State of Victoria treated the young girl from the Ouachitas and her legendary bronc riding husband as royalty. Pete and Babe had discovered a fairy-tale existence, and their happiness with their lives could not have been brighter. For Babe, her life with Pete was a magical carpet-ride of endless socializing with good friends, a high zest for living, and being able to afford everything she desired. For Pete, life was perfect in every way, and he did all he could to share that happiness with those around him.

13

International Rodeo Hero

By 1934, Pete Knight was one of the most revered showmen in Canada, England, Australia, and the United States. In a meteoric rise to stardom, Pete had truly become a legend in his own time.

In honor of Pete, Wilf Carter, a popular Canadian country singer and songwriter, wrote and recorded "Pete Knight – The King of the Cowboys" in Montreal on October 18, 1934. Pete and Wilf had met and become friends a year earlier at the Calgary Stampede in 1933, when Wilf had entered the wild horse race event as an 'ear-downer.'

Wilf, better known in the United States by his stage-name, 'Montana Slim,' arrived in Alberta in 1933, intent upon making a name for himself, after leaving his family home in Nova Scotia as a young boy. Having made himself familiar as an official songster in the company of the prestigious 'Trail Riders of the Canadian Rockies' and spending years perfecting his own style of yodelling, Wilf Carter became famous to western Canadians and American. His voice was heard on live radio throughout North America during 'the hungry thirties.'

Despite aspirations of becoming a 'star' in the wild horse race event, Wilf valued Pete's opinion. When Pete encouraged the young Nova Scotian to concentrate on singing, and leave the danger of the infield to others, Wilf promised the famous cowboy that he'd bow out if he couldn't make the grade as a contestant. Wilf was injured and muddied after attempting to ear-down a horse in the three-man event, and overall he was an unsuccessful contestant. He kept his word to his new-found friend, and focused on his singing career. Wilf Carter's tribute to Pete Knight was not simply an accolade to the great bronc rider, but a heartfelt thanks to the cowboy who saved 'Montana Slim' for a career that would eventually lead to music hall recording fame.

In a memorable celebration held in New York for Pete and Babe, in the autumn of 1934, Wilf sang his new song for the riding legend. When Wilf finished his song, the room erupted in an avalanche of cheering and back-slapping, by the many friends attending the party. From the grip of the bronc rider's handshake and the unforgettable response to the tribute that Wilf gave to Pete, it was several minutes before the legendary yodeller had enough feeling in his fingers to pick his guitar and sing another song for the applauding crowd.

After leaving New York, Pete and Babe wintered in Arkansas until March of 1935, when they travelled to Texas and returned to the rodeo trail. From Fort Worth, Pete and Babe headed west to California, and rode the rodeo circuit along the length of the state. It was during that early summer that Pete and Babe learned that Pete was once again voted 'World Champion Bronc Rider' for a third time. With the accolade came another cash prize, and another trophy saddle. From California, the couple headed northeast to the tough competition favored on the Nevada circuit.

The 1935 Reno Rodeo opened that year on Tuesday, July 2, with the most notorious bucking horse in the contest being *Harrison Dempsey*. Pete was favored to win in the three-day event. Three weeks earlier, he had mastered the acclaimed bucker at southern California's Gilroy Rodeo and won the contest. In an interview provided to a *Reno Evening Gazette* reporter, Pete's modesty shone through when he claimed that *Harrison Dempsey* had been a tough horse to ride, and only good luck had allowed him to win on the lively bronc. Of the one hundred twenty five bucking horses featured in Reno for the performance, *Bloody Island, Billy the Kid, Major Lou,* and *New Deal* all drew top billing as being formidable in their class.

Pete took third-place money behind Turk Greenough and Burrel Mulker, with Pete's good friends Cecil Henley and Earvin Collins receiving noteworthy mention of their riding skill in the competition. When the Reno Rodeo ended, Pete collected his winnings, said goodbye to his many friends, and he and Babe once again took to the highway, this time, bound for Winnemucca.

At the tenth annual Winnemucca Rodeo held at the end of August 1935, Pete won the bucking horse event in a three-day rodeo, presided over by Judge Maxwell McNutt of San Mateo County, California. Judge McNutt was the President of the Rodeo Association of America (RAA), and maintained a great friendship and huge respect for the young Alberta cowboy, whose riding skill thrilled thousands of spectators from Nevada, California, Oregon, and Idaho. As the RAA President and his wife cheered the bronc rider on, Pete's horse fell in the swirling infield dust. With a quick, fluid, and long rehearsed motion, Pete rolled clear of the tumbling horse. The dust-covered cowboy was offered a re-ride for the next afternoon.

Although the observers tallying the points were convinced Pete had won the bucking event, the trophy and prize money were awarded to Clay Carr of Visalia, California. Several officials and contestants in the rodeo submitted a protest against Carr's so-called championship. The rodeo committee reexamined the judges' score cards and discovered that Pete had indeed been the winner of the event. While the controversy spilled over into the press, Pete and Clay, who were friends but keen competitors, had already moved on to Nampa, Idaho, to compete in another rodeo, and were not fully aware of the outcry. The Winnemucca championship was subsequently handed to Pete, without affecting the friendship between the two highly-respected riders.

During the third week of February, 1936, the Rodeo Association of America held its eighth annual convention in the city of Tucson, Arizona. Well-known contestants from a dozen states and Canada's western provinces, along with wives and sweethearts, attended the prestigious rodeo gala. Harry Knight, who had endured many months of agonizing recovery after being trampled in Chicago, had since returned to bronc riding competition, and met up with Pete and Babe at the RAA convention.

For the fourth time, Pete Knight was again voted 'World Champion Bronc Rider.' Pete was also declared runner-up 'Grand Champion Cowboy' at that year's convention, second only to Arizona's Everett Bowman. In Tucson, Pete and Babe enjoyed several days of dining, dancing and 'talking shop' with the leading personalities of rodeo in North America, before hitting the rodeo trail for the beginning of yet another season.

As in the years before, Pete and Babe crossed the southwestern United States from Arizona to Texas, and then headed west to California. Travelling to Hayward, Pete and Babe spent several days visiting with their old friend, Harry Rowell, before Pete entered Harry's Hayward Rodeo, and won the bucking event. From central California, the rodeo circuit took the young couple north and east again, to Nevada.

The 1936 Reno Rodeo began with a ten thirty a.m. parade on Friday, July 3. Pete and Babe Knight were chosen to judge the parade's rider-and-horse entries. The Knights were assisted in this enjoyable task by an elegant young woman from California named Ruth Mix Knight, the woman Harry had recently married. At the end of the three-day rodeo, Pete was declared the winner of the bucking event, followed by Eddie and Pat Woods, Harry Knight, and 'Fritz' Truan.

In the late summer of 1936, Pete and Babe drove north to Canada to visit with Pete's family at Crossfield. Pete had kept his farm, as well as a growing string of bucking and dray horses. These he kept fed and foddered in Walt's corrals. Robert's older sons hovered around their famous uncle and gracious aunt, and listened intently to the exciting stories their Uncle Pete shared with them. Pete patiently answered their many questions about rodeos, bucking horses, and all the exciting places their travels had taken them.

While looking over a small herd of horses at Robert's farm one morning, Pete offered his expert advice to Raymond on how to handle and ride one of the green-broke saddle ponies. Lofting himself into the saddle, Pete bucked the horse across the corral, riding with balanced, 'rocking chair' ease as the pony tried and failed to dump him. Once during the extended visit, Pete and Babe went out on the open range with the boys, taking .22 rifles and boxes of ammunition for an afternoon of 'gopher hunting.' To the boys' surprise, Babe was an excellent shot with a rifle. The petite bride of the famous bronc rider 'drilled' a dozen targets from the open window of their coupe, as the car moved slowly across the prairie with Pete at the wheel. He marveled at her skill, and, laughing hysterically, offered his encouragement to his pretty wife. After awhile, the couple switched places and Pete, who was an equally adept marksman, fired away at distant targets as Babe maneuvered the car around the prevalent badger holes. The boys in the back seat were enthralled, as they took their turns potting away at targets from within the car. The afternoon's practice reduced the rodent infestation on the farm, and was especially useful for Raymond, who would find himself conscripted to fight a war a few years later. For the Knight boys it had been a brilliant, shining day of merriment on the open prairie with their Uncle Pete and Aunt Babe. The day finished with a large supper, all of the family present in Robert's home.

When the meal ended, the men smoked, discussed horses, farms, and grain prices, while the women washed the dishes and talked about gardening, fine linen, and bone china. As daylight slowly faded, Pete and Babe stood by their coupé and said their goodbyes to the older couples. The young Knight boys and girls leaned on the fenders of the shiny new car, fidgeting and jockeying for a better place to stand and get a better view of Pete and Babe. Hugs and smiles were exchanged, laughter and small tidbits of advice given. No one could possibly have known this was Pete's last goodbye to his family.

Soon Pete will be back on the rodeo circuit, the easy-going country life far behind.
Photo source:
Harold Knight Collection

14
A Cowboy's Right

On the twelfth of September, 1936, Pete Knight was awarded the Pendleton Round-up's 'Sam Jackson Trophy' for top "All-Around" honors, in recognition of his competitive showmanship and exceptional skill in the Bronc riding event. After Pendleton, Pete and Babe rode on to Nevada, arriving in the bustling centre of Winnemucca for that city's eleventh annual rodeo. Pete won first prize in the professional bucking horse contest, with the citizens of Humboldt county cheering their hero on. For the first time in his long, almost exclusively horse-mounted riding career, Pete entered in the Brahma steer-riding event, and won first-place day-money in the wild horse race, as well.

From Nevada, Pete and Babe headed east again, arriving in New York in time for the 1936 Madison Square Gardens Rodeo. The total prize money being offered at the two-week event was nearly thirty thousand dollars. Once again, cowboys from across North America were arriving in the eastern seaboard city, to compete in the prestigious affair.

In a quiet moment after an evening performance at the Gardens, Babe quietly told Pete that she was pregnant, and he was overjoyed with the news. Babe was sure the baby would arrive some time in April. They decided when rodeo season was over, it would be best for them to spend the winter in Arkansas, near Babe's parents.

When the rodeo ended in New York City, the happy couple moved on once again, to Boston. The Boston Gardens Rodeo of November 3, 1936, was the first time that cowboys walked out on a rodeo performance. While rodeo organizers at Madison Square Gardens had offered a fair share of the proceeds, Boston's producer, Colonel W .T. Johnson, offered less than a quarter of that. For the continent's top contestants – all having to travel more than a thousand miles to the show at their own expense, or having to endure the ignominy of travelling on a train provided by the producer – was a slap in the face, for any self-respecting cowboy.

Pete Knight was one of sixty-one contestants who formed the backbone of the protest, most of these cowboys later creating the *Cowboy Turtle Association.* They chose to call themselves *Turtles,* because a turtle is single-minded, stubborn, and impervious to punishment. Despite his usual easy-going manner, in moments when cowboys were treated unfairly, Pete's temper was one of the first to flare.

Colonel Johnson initially refused to increase the prize-money for contestants, and attempted to fill their positions with locally-hired pick-up men, horse groomers, and other 'extras.' Early in the week, Johnson fired Bob Crosby, a competent and trusted rodeo judge. Crosby – a highly regarded cowboy by all contestants – was the holder of the Theodore Roosevelt Trophy, awarded to the top 'All-Around' cowboy at both Pendleton and Cheyenne for three consecutive years. Two pick-up men who had openly expressed their support for the striking contestants were also fired. The rodeo's promoter made a determined attempt to recruit more than one hundred forty other cowboy contestants, who had competed in Chicago that autumn. Boston's contestants, however, had second-guessed Johnson's move, and had sent out telegrams to the Chicago rodeo, advising all contestants of the boycott. In an act of solidarity to the Boston contestants, the cowboys from the Chicago show responded in writing with a pledge of solidarity to the Cowboy Turtles in Boston. Having experienced the tough, dangerous nature of following the rodeo trail, often with little to show at the end of the day, the contestants from the windy city refused to cross the picket-line against legends such as Pete Knight, Herb Myers, Everett Bowman, the Canada Kid, Herman Linder, Eddie Curtis, Hub Whiteman, and a long list of other renowned cowboys.

As Boston spectators began arriving for the performance, the striking cowboys bought tickets to the show and sat in the stands, jeering and booing as Johnson rode onto the infield at the head of his grand parade. Pete sat in the stands with Babe, who was cat-calling and jeering as hard he was. When the performance began, every paying patron soon realized that the contest was being carried out by a group of non-cowboys. Every contestant was quickly thrown from real bucking horses, long before the completion of each ride. A disgruntled crowd began to shout from the Gardens' seats, "Bring on the real cowboys!" and the cowboys seated in the stadium fueled the momentum of the crowd's demand. As the evening's protest continued, a squad of Boston City Police arrived to quell the disturbance, led by Boston Police Sergeant Mike Carr, who warned the protesters to cease and desist, while at the same time expressing his sympathy for their cause.

In the midst of the bedlam, the Gardens' Band struck up the "The Star-Spangled Banner," bringing the muted cowboys and Bostonians to their feet. This quick action appeared to silence the protest, but in an instant of indecision, the bandleader led into a rendition of "Empty Saddles in the Old Corral," and the allusion to the absence of real cowboys in the rodeo was not lost on anyone. The 'strikers' belted out the words to the favorite western tune. Soon, every spectator was singing the familiar trail-song in support of the contestants, and when the singing ended the crowd renewed its vocal demand for 'real cowboys.' With boot-stomping, hand-clapping rhythm, the crowd continued to chant, "Bring on the cowboys! Bring on the cowboys!" and finally, Colonel Johnson relented. A meeting was held on the infield between the producer and the striking contestants, while thousands of spectators awaited the outcome from their seats. Members of the Boston Police continued their vigil, as fans continued to call for real cowboys. In less than fifteen minutes, a contestant spokesman announced to the paying fans that they would indeed ride, as their demands had just been met by Colonel Johnson. A cheer went up through the stands, and applause rolled through the building. The band-leader once again led his orchestra, this time in a fast-paced rendition of "My Pony Boy." On the next afternoon, after receiving an assurance in writing that a fair share of the proceeds would come their way in daily winnings and grand prizes, the cowboys of the Boston Gardens Rodeo put on a spectacular show for their returning fans, the likes of which Boston never saw again.

The following spring, the first annual meeting of the *Cowboy Turtle Association* convened in Fort Worth, coinciding with the opening of the Fort Worth Rodeo. Everett Bowman was elected President of the association, with Herman Linder taking office as First Vice-President. Harry Knight became the representative for the bronc riders and Pete Knight, although retaining an ordinary founding membership, provided good advice to other contestants who had aspirations of riding in unfamiliar territory across the United States.

As the Fort Worth show ended, Pete wished his friends well as he prepared to leave for California and the many rodeos he planned to attend in the western state that spring. One of the last of Pete's old friends to say goodbye to him was Herman Linder, who was heading home to southern Alberta for spring seeding. Herman long remembered their last parting, and his best recollection of Pete would always be his firm handshake, his generous smile, and his insistence on being neatly dressed – when he wasn't being tossed across an infield in levis, chaps, and spurs.

15

Honor to the King

Pete was planning to compete in a long list of rodeos across California, and having many friends living in towns from Burbank to the Canadian border, he considered taking up seasonal residence in the state. In early May, after riding in the 'Mother Lode Rodeo' in Sonora, California, Pete was headed for the small town of Hayward, east of San Francisco where his good friend Harry Rowell bought bucking horses and held an annual rodeo. Pete and Babe had every reason to celebrate that spring. In April of 1937, after an uncomplicated delivery in Hot Springs, Babe gave birth to a healthy baby girl and christened her "Deanna Thomasine." Once the baby was old enough to accompany her parents on the road, Babe and Deanna travelled to California to join Pete, and caught up with him at Merced, before the opening of the Hayward rodeo.

Hayward was a prosperous agricultural community with a thriving business centre and a deep sense of commitment to civic growth. Harry Rowell's rodeo provided the town with a sense of frontier nostalgia and had become a destination – a Mecca as well as a season's beginning – for the cream of the cowboy contestant crop across North America. Pete's old friend, Harry Knight, was also competing at the Hayward Rodeo, and greeted Babe and the month-old baby Deanna with the forthright affection of an adopted brother, brother-in-law, and 'Dutch Uncle.'

Pete, Babe and little Deanna had been sitting through the afternoon with several family friends, including their long-time friend, Amanda Crooks. When it came time for Pete to go, he handed his daughter to one of the ladies in their company. "I'll be right back," he said, and strode over to the chutes and made his way to the chute where *Duster*, the horse he drew that afternoon, awaited an unwanted rider. Pete saddled up the horse, tightened the cinch and patted the horse, then waited for the call from the judges.

Pete had kicked out on *Duster* several times in previous years, and knew the horse's quirks as well as anyone else who had ridden him. *Duster* had the reputation of being a good bucker, and would often dump his rider unexpectedly in the middle of the infield after a sudden, downward thrust of his head. He wasn't rated as spectacular a horse as *Gravedigger, Five Minutes to Midnight, Invalid,* or the well-known *Midnight.* 'A good, steady bucker' was the horse's overall assessment.

With his name and contestant number and the horse's name and the chute number being announced, Pete dropped into the saddle with a smooth, practiced motion, finding his stirrups as the horse became agitated with the additional weight on its back. With a quick nod from Pete, the chute-man swung the gate open.

The horse took his first great leap out past the plane of the chute, and Pete dug his spurs into the horse's shoulders. The ride was a balanced, choreographed performance, in the first, second, and third leap. Horse and rider charged across the infield in a small semi-circle of flying hooves and flashing spurs. The three judges smiled, already marking the rider down as a winner, for Pete had performed an exceptional ride in the first few seconds after leaving the chute and this ride appeared to be as good as the winning ride he had performed at the rodeo the previous year.

Suddenly, *Duster* snapped his head down and pulled Pete clean out of the saddle, his fist still gripping the buck-rein. In his typical fashion, the horse dropped Pete into the infield dust. Normally, a horse galloped away after dumping his rider, but *Duster* was still bucking hard and Pete was on his back in the infield dirt, facing the sky as the horse hovered above him. In the time-frozen moment where reason understood impending disaster, but could do nothing physically to avert it, *Duster* swung ever so slightly to his left, coming down with full force on Pete's chest before leaping away, the inertia of more than a thousand pounds being directed and focused into the tips of both hooves. The rider's ribs crushed beneath the onslaught.

Pick-up men were yelling and spurring their ponies to assist and cowboys were running onto the infield to offer what help they could. After a mad dash across the infield, Harry Knight was beside Pete in an instant, offering help and asking his friend if he was hurt.

"Yes," Pete said and winced at the effort it took to speak. "You're darned right I'm hurt!" He was gasping to get his breath, and his face was stricken a sickly grey. However, Pete insisted on regaining his feet and slowly walked back to the chutes without assistance. In the tradition of the rodeo, five thousand spectators who sat in the Hayward grandstand gave Pete a round of applause as he gravely crossed the infield at a slow, measured pace. His consciousness drifted into a dark swirl of quiet uncertainty and Pete fell to the ground beside the corral railing. He listened to the cheering and as the haze overtook his senses, the accolades faded away for the very last time.

Willing hands carried Pete to a waiting ambulance. A friend of Babe's, Mrs. Crooks promised she would take care of Deanna, while Babe was quietly spirited to a waiting car and driven to Hayward.

At the hospital, Babe found Pete lying on a gurney in the emergency room. He was conscious and lucid, and he smiled when he saw her. Pete was masking his pain as well as he could, and he told her not to fret, that he just needed to rest awhile. "Don't worry," he said. "I'll be fine." Pete closed his eyes, and within minutes, he stopped breathing. Babe kissed his face, brushed the hair from his forehead, and held tight to his hand, fervently praying for him to be well again.

Pete Knight died, still wearing his boots. His family and legions of men and women from across the entire continent mourned his passing. Pete had been their acclaimed "King" in deed, in song, and in legend. He would be remembered and spoken of with nothing less than reverence, his Stetson the symbol of his sovereignty. Pete Knight would forever remain . . . the Cowboy King.

Pete Knight's Last Ride
Hayward, California. May 23, 1937
Mere seconds after this photo of Pete riding *Duster* was snapped, tragedy struck. Milliseconds
from an 8 second ride, at a time when 10 seconds were required for a qualifying ride, Pete was
thrown and trampled by the frenzied horse, ending the reign of the Cowboy King.
Photo source: Marianne Beauregard – The Harry Rowell Family

Epilogue

Cowboys from across North America came to Hayward to pay their last respects to Pete Knight. The town's business community shut down for an entire week, as tributes were paid and a man among men was eulogized, time and time again. The 'Stars and Stripes' hung at half-mast on every flag pole in Hayward, and throughout the surrounding county the tribute was repeated. Mourners stood among the giant pine trees on the cemetery hill overlooking Hayward. Hundreds of friends and admirers of Pete's stood around the grave and wept, as his casket was slowly lowered, while Harry Knight stood quietly beside Babe, both weeping.

The shock of Pete Knight's passing never ended for Babe, for Pete's family, and for a long line of cowboys who continued to revere the memory of Pete Knight, even as they themselves grew old and passed away. Urban Guichon - who would in time marry Eneas McCormick's daughter and inherit Riley & McCormick Saddlery - was then living on his father's Douglas Lake ranch, in British Columbia. As that May week began in 1937, Urban remembered his father's foreman sitting down to breakfast and quietly relating in measured tones that the radio news had announced Pete Knight's death. In a tribute of silence, nobody at the Guichon ranch spoke for the rest of the morning.

Harold Knight believed his Uncle Pete to be invincible. When his cousin Bob announced Pete's death on that May afternoon, Harold initially thought that Bob was talking about his own brother Pete, and not their famous uncle.

State representatives from over half of the United States, and all of Canada's provincial governments sent flowers to Pete Knight's funeral, until they numbered in the tens of thousands. Pete's coffin and the entire room around it was wreathed in a floral tribute to his legendary grandeur.

Wilf Carter recorded "Pete Knight's Last Ride" in New York later that year, but the song was not as popular as his 1934 recording of "Pete Knight: The King of the Cowboys."

The National Cowboy & Western Heritage Museum in Oklahoma City, USA, inducted Pete Knight as a rodeo honoree in their Hall of Fame in 1958. The "Horseman's Hall of Fame" was later dedicated at the Calgary Brewery and Salt-water Aquarium by Sandy Cross. Featured among its many exhibits was a barn scene with life-size figures of rodeo legends Dick Cosgrave, Clem Gardner, Herman Linder and Pete Knight. The "Horseman's Hall of Fame" closed its doors in 1972, after the brewery was purchased by Carling-O'keefe, and the exhibits were dismantled and dispersed. A Wax Museum opened its doors in Banff, Alberta, early in 1964, featuring a Calgary Stampede scene bearing wax figures of Pete Knight, Guy Weadick, Charlie Russell, and Wilf Carter in one of its galleries. The museum faded from Banff's list of attractions in the early 1970's. Eneas McCormick continued the line of Pete Knight chaps, and his successor, Urban Guichon, honored the pledge made by Eneas, until Riley & McCormick downsized its operation and closed its factory. Brave little Crossfield, with its four-block-long Main Street and grain elevator row that would soon vanish, decreed that its memorial arena be named after Pete Knight, more than forty years after his death. On June 25, 1977, the "Pete Knight Memorial Centre" was dedicated. Babe Knight, Wilf Carter, more than one hundred members of the Knight family, and one hundred more aging cowboys - the last of Pete's surviving friends from across Alberta and the western United States - gathered to pay tribute to Pete Knight and to name the Crossfield centre in honor of the legendary cowboy. In 1979, with the dedication of the 'Hall of Fame' at Colorado Springs, Pete Knight was inducted into the ProRodeo Hall of Fame and Museum of the American Cowboy. The Canadian Rodeo Historical Society - established in 1980, at Cochrane, Alberta - inducted Pete Knight into the Canadian Rodeo Hall of Fame as the society's first honoree, followed by *Midnight*, the first 'horse-inductee.'

In 1960, Pete's mortal remains were moved to Hot Springs, Arkansas, where Babe lived for the rest of her life. She often took flowers to Pete's grave in the silence of the cemetery, while speaking softly of their past together. Deanna was married in Hot Springs, gave birth to a daughter and a son, and then died after contracting cancer in 1982. Babe Knight passed away from old age in 1987; both Babe and Deanna are buried beside Pete at the Greenwood Cemetery, in Hot Springs, Arkansas, for all time, beneath a huge oak tree.

The Prince of Wales Cup, the Dempsey Trophy and a long list of other trophies, saddles, bridles, boots, gold belt-buckles and photographs now rest as national treasures in the Cowboy Hall of Fame in Oklahoma City, mere yards from the enshrined remains of the bucking horse *Midnight*, the legendary gelding having died in 1936, in Denver, Colorado.

Pete Knight was one of the finest Goodwill Ambassadors that Canada ever had, and his character and spirit were equally matched by his outstanding ability to ride bucking horses in the international arena.

Pete's good friend and fellow competitor, Herman Linder - acclaimed as "Canada's Mr. Rodeo," legendary bronc rider, and a recipient of the 'Order of Canada' for his many contributions to rodeo - often stated that Pete Knight "was one of the greatest, if not the greatest bronc rider that ever lived."

Appendix A

The Rules of the Rodeo Association of America

(Published in the Nevada State Journal, Sunday, 30 June 1935)

1. The management reserves the right to reject the entry of any contestant who has violated the general rules, who has been dishonest in competition or who has proven to be undesirable at any recognized rodeo.

2. All contestants are required to read the rules carefully, particularly those relating to the contests or events in which they enter. Failure to understand rules will not be accepted as an excuse.

3. The management assumes no responsibility or liability for injury or damage to the person, property or stock of any owner, contestant or assistant. Each participant, by the act of his entry, waives all claim against the management for injuries he, or his property, may sustain.

4. The Timers, Judges and all other officials shall be appointed by the management and their decision will be final in all matters relating to the contests in which they are called to officiate.

5. Contestants should be at place indicated by management when drawings for horses and places are held. If they are not present, either in person or by representative, the management will name someone to draw for them and contestants must accept the selection made.

6. Numbers will be furnished by management to all contestants and numbers must be displayed so as to be visible to spectators and Judges.

7. Contestants must be on hand to answer call of arena director and must comply with all other rules of the management of each particular contest or exhibition. When, in the opinion of the arena directors, a sufficient number of contestants are present for an event, there will be no delay because other contestants are not present.

8. Substitutes will not be permitted in any event or contest.

9. Requests for withdrawal from any event or contest and the return of entrance fee will be passed on by the management and such requests will not be considered (except in case of injury to contestant) unless made at least one day in advance.

10. The management may withdraw any contestant's name and entry, debar him from any or all events and withhold any money due him, for violation of any of the governing rules or rules of the Judges, or for any of the following offenses:

- Refusing to contest on animal drawn by or selected for him.
- Being under the influence of liquor.
- Rowdyism (sic); mistreatment of stock.
- Altercation with Judges or officials.

11. All contestants must participate in down town parades and grand entries.

Horse and rider rated separately on basis of 100 percent.

Percentage of both horse and rider to be added and divided by two, thus indicating final rating.

Chart or sheet should also show position from which the Judge observed the ride, to wit: right, left, front or rear.

Appendix B

The Rules of the Saddle Bronc Bucking Event

(Canada) The rules governing the Saddle Bronc Riding event were first formalized in print during the 1930's, with the advent of the Cowboy Turtle Association in the United States and with the formation of the Cowboys' Protective Association in Canada. The Canadian Stampede Manager's Association gave its stamp of approval to the following rules, as are found in the Canadian Rodeo Rules Handbook of 1956: Contest Rules Saddle Bronc Riding

Riders and horses for each day will be selected by Management; horses to be furnished by management and riders will draw for mounts. If rider draws a horse he has once ridden during a contest, he must draw again. Contestants must ride as often, and on any horse judges may deem necessary to determine winner. Riding to be done with plain halter, ONE rein and saddle. Each contestant must supply his own cotton rope or plaited cotton rein, not more than 1 ½ inches in diameter, which must pass the inspection of the chute judges. Management will supply halter. Saddle may be supplied by either management or contestant, but must be regulation Association saddle. Riding rein and hand must be on same side. The rein shall be loose at one end and not knotted, and the rider shall not insert fingers in plaiting.

Horses to be saddled in chute or arena as management may direct. Rider will place saddle and ensure that it remains properly centred. Outside of this, rider will have nothing whatever to do with saddling. Management will be responsible for cinching and flanking. Rider will be disqualified if he allows anyone to pull up on back of saddle as horse is being cinched or interfere in any way with saddling other than placing saddle. In case cinch was not tight enough and saddle comes off, contestant will be given re-ride, judges to decide what horse he will get for re-ride.

To qualify, rider must have spurs over shoulders and touching horse when horse's front feet hit the ground first jump out of the chute, and rider must continue to spur throughout the ride to the satisfaction of the judges. Rider must leave starting place with rein in one hand, the other hand high in the air, and must keep free hand in air at all times. Rein hand must be absolutely free, showing daylight as he leaves chute.

No horse shall be turned loose until rider indicates he is ready. Ten seconds will be given by timers with stop watches from flag until whistle, to each rider. Should a horse fall and if, in the opinion of the judges, the animal was not pulled down or over by the rider, his ride shall be judged up to the time the horse fell; and if the judges so decide, they may permit a re-ride.

OFFENCES - The following offences will disqualify a contestant.

- Not spurring a horse high enough in the shoulders first jump out of chutes.
- Losing stirrup.
- Failing to be ready when name is called.
- Being bucked off.
- Changing hands on rein.
- Not giving horse its head upon leaving starting place.
- Pulling leather.
- Abusing or fighting horse.
- Slapping horse.
- Any attempt upon the part of contestant to violate or take unfair advantage of the rules.
- The taping, excessive resining, gumming, wetting, or oiling any part of the rider's equipment or clothing, tacks in boots, or stirrups, in an endeavor to assist rider.

JUDGES: There will be two judges to judge the actual riding. One of these judges shall judge all riders on left side, one on right side. The decisions of these judges shall be absolutely final. Management will appoint such other officials as chute judges, flagmen, etc., as are deemed necessary for the successful operation of the contest.

Averaging rides and horses. Each judge shall mark the percentage he gives each rider and horse, as he witnesses their performance from his own position, without consulting the other judge. Each judge turns his slip covering each ride in to field clerk, who will figure percentages from records turned into him by the judges. Percentage of both horse and rider on each judge's card to be added to obtain each judge's rating. No erasers can be used by judges. If change in figures is necessary, line should be drawn through original figure and substitute figure written above.

The Rules of Saddle Bronc Riding found forty-five years later, in the current Professional Rodeo and Rules," have changed very little since the beginning of formal Rodeo Competition in Western Canada, and are listed as follows:

Saddle Bronc Riding

1. Horse to be furnished by the producer (of the rodeo). Riding to be done with plain halter, one-rope rein, and standard Association saddle. Stock contractor may call on judges to pass on whether or not a saddle is standard.

2. Stock Contractors must furnish their own halters and contestants must use them. Placing of buckrein, foreign material, fitness of halter, etc., subject to judges' approval. (a) Standard halter must be used unless agreement is made by both contestant and stock contractor. (b) If halter breaks during ride, rider shall be given a reride on the same horse, provided halter is not supplied by contestant.

3. Horses to be saddled in chute. Saddles may not be set too far ahead on horse's withers. Rider may cinch own saddle, or examine same, to determine if satisfactory. Either stock contractor or contestant shall have the right to call the judge to pass on whether or not horse is properly saddled and flanked to buck its best. (a) Middle flank belongs to rider, but contractor may have rider put flank cinch behind curve of horse's belly. Flank cinch may be hobbled (with a light piece of twine, to the cinch forward). (b) Contestants may cinch saddle from either side.

4. Unless animal stalls, no horse can be hotshotted after the rider sits down, and then only at the request of the contestant.

5. To qualify, rider must have spurs over the break of the shoulders and touching horse when horse's front feet hit the ground first jump out of the chute. One arm and hand must be free at all times.

6. Saddle bronc riding shall be timed for eight (8) seconds; time to start when animals inside front shoulder passes the plane of the chute.

7. Any of the following offences shall disqualify a rider: being bucked off; changing hands on rein; wrapping rein around hand; losing stirrup; touching animal, equipment or person with free hand; riding with locked rowels, or rowels that will lock on spurs; failing to follow judges' instructions when horse stalls in the chute; for using any substance except dry rosin on saddle or chaps; losing or dropping rein during ride.

8. Contest Saddle Specifications:

(a) Rigging: ¾ double - front edge of D-ring must not pull further back than directly below centre of point of swell. Standard E-Z or ring type saddle must be used and cannot exceed five and three quarter inches (5 ¾") outside-width measurement.

(b) Swell Undercut: Not more than two inches (2") - one inch (1") on each side.

(c) Gullet: Not less than four inches (4") wide at centre of fork of covered saddle.

(d) Tree: Saddles must be built on standard tree.

(e) Specifications: Fork - fourteen inches (14") wide; height - nine inches (9") maximum; gullet - five and three quarter inches (5 ¾") wide; cantle - five inches (5") maximum height, fourteen inches (14") maximum width.

(f) Stirrup leathers must be hung over bars.

(g) Saddle should conform to the above measurements with a reasonable added thickness for leather covering.

(h) No freaks allowed (no freak or odd saddles).

(i) Cinches must be at least five inches (5") wide.

Other rules pertaining to the handling of stock and to rerides were included, in the intervening seventy-year period. Someone would have to turn the contestant's horse out, and the horse's halter could not be held. Fines beginning at $25 and escalating with each offence could be imposed, for delay and other infractions deemed to be excessive or unnecessary. The awarding of a re-ride would be decided upon at the discretion of the judges, and could not be asked for by the contestant. Despite the simplicity of the rules, and there being little more than a page and a half of them to adhere to, some of the toughest and most experienced riders in North America would be physically challenged in every contest they entered. The risk involved, in attempting to make a winning ride on an unpredictable bucking horse, could result in serious injury or death to a rider, after just one slip made by contestant or mount.

Appendix C

Pete Knight The King of the Cowboys
by Wilf Carter

(spoken)
Here's a song about the greatest cowboy ever crawled aboard a saddle...
Pete Knight, The 'King' of the Cowboys!
(lyrics sung)
Just listen awhile to my story, 'bout a lad from the wide-open plain,
who has won a great name the world over, Pete Knight, 'King' of rodeo fame,
He was raised at Crossfield, Alberta --- just a little cowtown in the west,
Unless he was out 'mongst the broncos, it seemed he was never at rest!
He took a real love for the saddle, like most of us boys in the west,
How he'd watch those cowboys a'riding, on Sunday it seemed was the best,
One day he cornered a bronco, just using a sack for a blind,
Stuck on a saddle, pulled away the blind, yelled "Cayuse, let's see you unwind!"
(Yodeling interlude)
From that day he made it a practice, each day a bronco to tame,
And now he's the 'King' of all cowboys, that ever set foot on the range,
He come out of the chute just a'kickin', both feet high up in the mane,
When the bronc did his best to unload him, the horse never lived he can't
tame!He has ridden in all of the Stampedes, a'going north, south, east and west,
At the World's Fair held in Chicago, he won the World's bronc riding contest!
But, Pete, like all other cowboys, a girl came into his life,
He took her hand at the alter, and made her his loving wife.
Canada's proud of her cowboy, who has won great honor and fame,
Let's take off our hats to the 'King' of them all,
Pete Knight, from the Alberta plain!
(Yodeling finalé)

Pete Knight's Last Ride
by Wilf Carter

It seems my whole life's full of heart-ache and sighs,
Always something to make me feel blue,
For I've just lost a pal, like a brother to me
Seems I can't believe that it's true.
Oh, we were old pals on the prairie, so gay,
Many times we have rode side by side,
Never dreaming a bronco would throw him,
And Pete Knight would take his last ride.
He was riding a bronco called "Slow-down,"
Many times he had spurred that old hide
But when he left the chute, fate played a hand,
That's when Pete took his last ride.

He'll still remain 'King' of the cowboys,

Many times he had won world-wide fame,
And millions of people who knew him
They all idolize Pete Knight's name.
It was only last fall that we parted, so gay,
His handshake I'll always recall;
When he said, "So long, Pal, good luck to you,
I'll see you the next coming fall."
But now I stand, head bowed in silence
And a tear-drop may fall unashamed,
We'll miss him a lot since he left us
Old memories will always remain.
Oh, some day there'll be a great round-up,
When the ranch-boss starts combing the plains,
May our names all be squared on the tally,
May we meet on that heavenly range.

Appendix D

McCulloch's Tribute to Pete Knight

Pete Knight's Final Ride

It was in 1937, five-ten that fateful day,
At Hayward, California, on the twenty-third of May.
And just to set some people straight on the bronc he rode that day,
It was an outlaw horse named Duster, that sent him on his way.
The Champ went off that bucking horse and fell beneath his feet,
Old Duster swung back to his left, that's when he trampled Pete.
A broken rib had punctured him as he jumped up on his feet,
Fate had dealt the cards to both but the cowboy drew defeat.
Harry Knight came out to lend a hand and the boys all gathered round,
But Pete cashed in before they took him through the gates of the infield ground.

Every word I've said is true…boys, I tell you so.
Twas in Harry Rowell's arena on that Sunday long ago.
A quiet country graveyard, just outside of town
The Lone Tree Cemetery is where they laid him down.
Up there in the Cowboy Hall of Fame, I am sure the Lord would write,
"World Champion Bronc Rider," beside the name "Pete Knight."

John D. McCulloch
Calgary, Alberta

Appendix E

The Linder's Tribute to Pete Knight

In Memory of our friend Pete Knight

My memory of "THE" staunch cowboy
is a friendly smile and a word of joy,
to all cowboys from either land
willing to help, was this great hand.
As a champion, he was unsurpassed,
during the years his riding did last;
None were too large; none too small
with his nerve of steel he'd challenge all.
From earthly cares he is now redeemed;
cruel to his friends it may have seemed.
But his Maker surely knew what was best,
when he took our dear friend away to rest.
He is gone beyond --- where good cowboys go;
When we shall meet him, we do not know.
So let our memories be what they shall,
Good they must be --- who knew him well.

Agnes & Herman Linder

Appendix F

Interviews

Billy Coates, 15 October, 1983.

Hank Freisen, 7 August, 1981.

Mary Guichon, 15 May 2003 and 10 June, 2003.

Urban Guichon, 29 August, 1981.

Fred Kennedy, 9 September, 1978.

Ida Lee 'Babe' Knight, 17 June, 1977 and 5 July, 1979

Harold Knight, 2 May, 2003, 22 July, 2003, 8 April, 2004

Raymond Knight, my life time to July, 2003.

Nellie (Knight) McClain, 6 December, 1975 and 20 July, 1982.

Frank Sharp, 5 May, 1979 and 14 August, 1983.

Bill Stroup, 2 June 2003.

Harry Vold, 11 May, 2003.

Dick West, 10 September, 1984.

Edwin Kulsky, 4 June, 2003

Theodore 'Teddy' Togstead, 6 April, 2004A

Secondary Sources

Carter, Wilf. *The Yodelling Cowboy*. Toronto, 1961.

Davis, Jim. *We remember . . . Pete Knight*. Calgary, 1976.

Faulknor, Cliff. *Turn Him Loose!* Saskatoon, 1977.

Kennedy, Fred. *The Calgary Stampede Story*. Calgary, 1952.

Kennedy, Fred, *Alberta Was My Beat*. Calgary, 1975.

Koller, Joe, *"Pete Knight's Death Ride," Golden West*. March, 1967.

MacEwan, Grant. *Pat Burns: Cattle King*. Saskatoon, 1979

Index